PLAY ON SHAKESPEARE

Richard III

T0345793

PLAY ON SHAKESPEARE

All's Well That Ends Well	Virginia Grise
Antony and Cleopatra	Christopher Chen
As You Like It	David Ivers
The Comedy of Errors	Christina Anderson
Coriolanus	Sean San José
Cymbeline	Andrea Thome
Edward III	Octavio Solis
Hamlet	Lisa Peterson
Henry IV	Yvette Nolan
Henry V	Lloyd Suh
Henry VI	Douglas P. Langworthy
Henry VIII	Caridad Svich
Julius Caesar	Shishir Kurup
King John	Brighde Mullins
King Lear	Marcus Gardley
Love's Labour's Lost	Josh Wilder
Macbeth	Migdalia Cruz
Measure for Measure	Aditi Brennan Kapil
The Merchant of Venice	Elise Thoron
The Merry Wives of Windsor	Dipika Guha
A Midsummer Night's Dream	Jeffrey Whitty
Much Ado About Nothing	Ranjit Bolt
Othello	Mfoniso Udofia
Pericles	Ellen McLaughlin
Richard II	Naomi Iizuka
Richard III	Migdalia Cruz
Romeo and Juliet	Hansol Jung
The Taming of the Shrew	Amy Freed
The Tempest	Kenneth Cavander
Timon of Athens	Kenneth Cavander
Titus Andronicus	Amy Freed
Troilus and Cressida	Lillian Groag
Twelfth Night	Alison Carey
The Two Gentlemen of Verona	Amelia Roper
The Two Noble Kinsmen	Tim Slover
The Winter's Tale	Tracy Young

Richard III

by
William Shakespeare

Modern verse translation by
Migdalia Cruz

Dramaturgy by
Ishia Bennison

ACMRS — Arizona Center for Medieval and Renaissance Studies

ACMRS PRESS

Arizona State University
Tempe, Arizona
2021

Publication of Play On Shakespeare is assisted by
generous support from the Hitz Foundation.
For more information, please visit www.playonshakespeare.org

Published by ACMRS Press
Arizona Center for Medieval and Renaissance Studies,
Arizona State University, Tempe, Arizona
www.acmrspress.com

Library of Congress Cataloging-in-Publication Data
Names: Cruz, Migdalia, author. | Bennison, Ishia, contributor. |
    Shakespeare, William, 1564-1616. King Richard III.
Title: Richard III / by William Shakespeare ; modern verse translation by
    Migdalia Cruz ; dramaturgy by Ishia Bennison.
Other titles: King Richard III
Description: Tempe, Arizona : ACMRS Press, 2021. | Series: Play on
    Shakespeare | Summary: "A contemporary English verse translation,
    faithfully keeping the poetry, the puns, and the politics of the play
    intact, with a rigorous and in-depth examination of Richard III-the
    man, the king, the outsider-who is still the only English king to have
    died in battle"-- Provided by publisher.
Identifiers: LCCN 2021017585 (print) | LCCN 2021017586 (ebook) | ISBN
    9780866986762 (paperback) | ISBN 9780866986779 (ebook)
Subjects: LCSH: Richard III, King of England, 1452-1485--Drama. | Great
    Britain--History--Richard III, 1483-1485--Drama.
Classification: LCC PR2878.K9 C78 2021 (print) | LCC PR2878.K9
    (ebook) | DDC 812/.54--dc23
LC record available at https://lccn.loc.gov/2021017585
LC ebook record available at https://lccn.loc.gov/2021017586

Printed in the United States of America

We wish to acknowledge our gratitude
for the extraordinary generosity of the
Hitz Foundation

∽

Special thanks to the Play on Shakespeare staff
Lue Douthit, CEO and Creative Director
Kamilah Long, Executive Director
Taylor Bailey, Associate Creative Director and Senior Producer
Summer Martin, Director of Operations
Amrita Ramanan as Senior Cultural Strategist and Dramaturg
Katie Kennedy, Publications Project Manager

∽

Originally commissioned by the
Oregon Shakespeare Festival
Bill Rauch, Artistic Director
Cynthia Rider, Executive Director

PLAY ON SHAKESPEARE

In 2015, the Oregon Shakespeare Festival announced a new commissioning program. It was called "Play on!: 36 playwrights translate Shakespeare." It elicited a flurry of reactions. For some people this went too far: "You can't touch the language!" For others, it didn't go far enough: "Why not new adaptations?" I figured we would be on the right path if we hit the sweet spot in the middle.

Some of the reaction was due not only to the scale of the project, but its suddenness: 36 playwrights, along with 38 dramaturgs, had been commissioned and assigned to translate 39 plays, and they were already hard at work on the assignment. It also came fully funded by the Hitz Foundation with the shocking sticker price of $3.7 million.

I think most of the negative reaction, however, had to do with the use of the word "translate." It's been difficult to define precisely. It turns out that there is no word for the kind of subtle and rigorous examination of language that we are asking for. We don't mean "word for word," which is what most people think of when they hear the word translate. We don't mean "paraphrase," either.

The project didn't begin with 39 commissions. Linguist John McWhorter's musings about translating Shakespeare is what sparked this project. First published in his 1998 book *Word on the Street* and reprinted in 2010 in *American Theatre* magazine, he notes that the "irony today is that the Russians, the French, and other people in foreign countries possess Shakespeare to a much greater extent than we do, for the simple reason that they get to enjoy Shakespeare in the language they speak."

This intrigued Dave Hitz, a long-time patron of the Oregon Shakespeare Festival, and he offered to support a project that looked at Shakespeare's plays through the lens of the English we speak today. How much has the English language changed since Shakespeare? Is it possible that there are conventions in the early modern English of Shakespeare that don't translate to us today, especially in the moment of hearing it spoken out loud as one does in the theater?

How might we "carry forward" the successful communication between actor and audience that took place 400 years ago? "Carry forward," by the way, is what we mean by "translate." It is the fourth definition of *translate* in the Oxford English Dictionary.

As director of literary development and dramaturgy at the Oregon Shakespeare Festival, I was given the daunting task of figuring out how to administer the project. I began with Kenneth Cavander, who translates ancient Greek tragedies into English. I figured that someone who does that kind of work would lend an air of seriousness to the project. I asked him how might he go about translating from the source language of early modern English into the target language of contemporary modern English?

He looked at different kinds of speech: rhetorical and poetical, soliloquies and crowd scenes, and the puns in comedies. What emerged from his tinkering became a template for the translation commission. These weren't rules exactly, but instructions that every writer was given.

First, do no harm. There is plenty of the language that doesn't need translating. And there is some that does. Every playwright had different criteria for assessing what to change.

Second, go line-by-line. No editing, no cutting, no "fixing." I want the whole play translated. We often cut the gnarly bits in

Shakespeare for performance. What might we make of those bits if we understood them in the moment of hearing them? Might we be less compelled to cut?

Third, all other variables stay the same: the time period, the story, the characters, their motivations, and their thoughts. We designed the experiment to examine the language.

Fourth, and most important, the language must follow the same kind of rigor and pressure as the original, which means honoring the meter, rhyme, rhetoric, image, metaphor, character, action, and theme. Shakespeare's astonishingly compressed language must be respected. Trickiest of all: making sure to work within the structure of the iambic pentameter.

We also didn't know which of Shakespeare's plays might benefit from this kind of investigation: the early comedies, the late tragedies, the highly poetic plays. So we asked three translators who translate plays from other languages into English to examine a Shakespeare play from each genre outlined in the *First Folio*: Kenneth took on *Timon of Athens,* a tragedy; Douglas Langworthy worked on the *Henry the Sixth* history plays, and Ranjit Bolt tried his hand at the comedy *Much Ado about Nothing.*

Kenneth's *Timon* received a production at the Alabama Shakespeare in 2014 and it was on the plane ride home that I thought about expanding the project to include 39 plays. And I wanted to do them all at once. The idea was to capture a snapshot of contemporary modern English. I couldn't oversee that many commissions, and when Ken Hitz (Dave's brother and president of the Hitz Foundation) suggested that we add a dramaturg to each play, the plan suddenly unfolded in front of me. The next day, I made a simple, but extensive, proposal to Dave on how to commission and develop 39 translations in three years. He responded immediately with "Yes."

My initial thought was to only commission translators who translate plays. But I realized that "carry forward" has other meanings. There was a playwright in the middle of the conversation 400 years ago. What would it mean to carry *that* forward?

For one thing, it would mean that we wanted to examine the texts through the lens of performance. I am interested in learning how a dramatist makes sense of the play. Basically, we asked the writers to create performable companion pieces.

I wanted to tease out what we mean by contemporary modern English, and so we created a matrix of writers who embodied many different lived experiences: age, ethnicity, gender-identity, experience with translations, geography, English as a second language, knowledge of Shakespeare, etc.

What the playwrights had in common was a deep love of language and a curiosity about the assignment. Not everyone was on board with the idea and I was eager to see how the experiment would be for them. They also pledged to finish the commission within three years.

To celebrate the completion of the translations, we produced a festival in June 2019 in partnership with The Classic Stage Company in New York to hear all 39 of them. Four hundred years ago I think we went to *hear* a play; today we often go to *see* a play. In the staged reading format of the Festival, we heard these plays as if for the first time. The blend of Shakespeare with another writer was seamless and jarring at the same time. Countless actors and audience members told us that the plays were understandable in ways they had never been before.

Now it's time to share the work. We were thrilled when Ayanna Thompson and her colleagues at the Arizona Center for Medieval and Renaissance Studies offered to publish the translations for us.

I ask that you think of these as marking a moment in time.

The editions published in this series are based on the scripts that were used in the Play on! Festival in 2019. For the purpose of the readings, there were cuts allowed and these scripts represent those reading drafts.

The original commission tasked the playwrights and dramaturg to translate the whole play. The requirement of the commission was for two drafts which is enough to put the ball in play. The real fun with these texts is when there are actors, a director, a dramaturg, and the playwright wrestling with them together in a rehearsal room.

The success of a project of this scale depends on the collaboration and contributions of many people. The playwrights and dramaturgs took the assignment seriously and earnestly and were humble and gracious throughout the development of the translations. Sally Cade Holmes and Holmes Productions, our producer since the beginning, provided a steady and calm influence.

We have worked with more than 1,200 artists in the development of these works. We have partnered with more than three dozen theaters and schools. Numerous readings and more than a dozen productions of these translations have been heard and seen in the United States as well as Canada, England, and the Czech Republic.

There is a saying in the theater that 80% of the director's job is taken care of when the production is cast well. Such was my luck when I hired Taylor Bailey, who has overseen every reading and workshop, and was the producer of the Festival in New York. Katie Kennedy has gathered all the essays, and we have been supported by the rest of the Play on Shakespeare team: Kamilah Long, Summer Martin, and Amrita Ramanan.

All of this has come to be because Bill Rauch, then artistic director of the Oregon Shakespeare Festival, said yes when Dave

Hitz pitched the idea to him in 2011. Actually he said, "Hmm, interesting," which I translated to "yes." I am dearly indebted to that 'yes.'

My gratitude to Dave, Ken, and the Hitz Foundation can never be fully expressed. Their generosity, patience, and unwavering belief in what we are doing has given us the confidence to follow the advice of Samuel Beckett: "Ever tried. Ever failed. No matter. Try again. Fail again. Fail better."

Play on!

Dr. Lue Douthit
CEO/Creative Director at Play on Shakespeare
October 2020

WHAT WAS I THINKING?

From Last Plantagenet King to Leicester Parking Lot Row R: Richard III & Me
By Migdalia Cruz

The outrageous idea was to look at revered texts by one of the most revered playwrights in the White Male Western Canon and help them speak to a 21st Century audience that includes everyone else — leaving intact the poetry and rhythms, place and characters.

This was Lue Douthit's (then a dramaturg at OSF, now the pragmatic and profound Creative Director of Play On Shakespeare) and Dave Hitz's (of the Hitz Foundation) idea. Create a revitalized canon that allowed for a modern ear to understand all of Shakespeare's original intentions without dumbing down the text or poetry.

How delicious, as a Puerto Rican woman from the Bronx, to become part of the Western Canon in this subversive way. If it worked, it could mean that people of color would become clearly entitled to these classic works, and, in a deeper way, entitled to poetry without question, explanation or rancor. So when Lue asked me, first to translate *Macbeth* and then *Richard III*, I said, "Yes."

After translating *Macbeth*, I found I missed the rigorous scholarship of deep-diving into Shakespeare (where, for example, is Cawdor and what is the etymology of thane?). I longed for a second project, but all the canon had already been assigned and there was little chance that I would get another assignment. But then, a miracle! The play about the (presumed) vicious Catholic English sovereign, *Richard III*, became available. As a fellow lapsed Catholic and, also, slightly vicious, it seemed like the perfect assignment for me. The powerless or the othered people seeking by any means to become powerful, and the fall of people who search for power without remembering the consequences of their actions — read like a Migdalia Cruz play to me.

I saw the direct link between Richard and Macbeth. *Richard III* was Shakespeare's fourth play (or sixth play depending on who you ask). A play written by a young writer still searching for his voice, whose poetry is not yet fully realized. I found that *Richard III* laid a foundation for his 28th play, *Macbeth*, a beautifully crafted and poetically precise play. Interestingly, I found that Shakespeare stole lines from himself in *Richard III* and placed them into *Macbeth*, as so many playwrights do. We repeat themes, steal feelings and relationships from past work that still haunts us. This further humanized this writer that I was attempting to infuse or reimagine from my own creative landscape.

For instance, in *R3*, Richard says before the murderer Tyrell enters:

> Murder her brothers, and then marry her.
> Uncertain way of gain. But I am in
> *So far in blood* that sin will pluck on sin.
> Tear-falling pity dwells not in this eye.

My translation:

> Murder the princes, and marry the princess.
> Unholy way to prosper. But I am
> *So steeped in blood* that sin will pluck out sin.
> Tear-dropping mercy dwells not in this eye.

And from *Macbeth*, Macbeth says after the Murderers have killed Banquo and his ghost has appeared to Macbeth at the banquet:

> All causes shall give way. I am in blood
> *Stepped in so far*, that should I wade no more,
> Returning were as tedious as go o'er.

My translation:

> Nothing shall halt my way. I am in blood
> *Stepped in so far*, that should I wade no further,
> Returning were as bloody as crossing o'er.

Finding parallels lines in *Richard III*, gave me insight into the writer Shakespeare would become — from plot-heavy history play writer to a stage-poet. It also was interesting to see how he developed his poetry and gave his characters more humanity over time.

Once I discovered these parallels, then I approached Richard as I would one of my own characters, by creating an altar for him and to the play: a spiritual collection of talismans, music, colors, or sacred objects that might have belonged to the characters, or a time in the character's life, or a place that is important to the character or to the story. To find items, thoughts, photographs for *Richard III*, I went to Bosworth Field to see where he died and then to Leicester to see where they found his body — in a car park that was once a Catholic church — in an area that was marked "R." I think he was determined to be found and given a proper burial. That "R" was no coincidence (see Fig. 1).

And then I visited his official tomb at Leicester Cathedral (see Fig. 2).

Next, I found Richard's soundtrack. For all my plays, I find the music of the characters and/or the music I need to hear to write them — music that somehow embodies them. For Richard, it was The Clash, especially "London Calling" and "London's Burning." I saw him as a punky rebel, that affected change by breaking through England's inertia — a hated outsider pushed to his ambitious fall by

Figure 1. The imprint of Richard's skeleton in his original grave under the Greyfriars' Catholic Church in Leicester, U.K., which became a car park. (*M. Cruz photo*.)

the cruelty around him.

Then, I went through videotapes from the RSC classes in speaking iambic pentameter led by John Barton. They're kind of outrageous, from the 1970s. Everyone is smoking — looks like they're talking in a fog. But it's interesting to see how they all — even famous British actors — struggle with the language. Part of

Figure 2. Richard III's tomb in Leicester Cathedral. (*M. Cruz photo.*)

the struggle with the language is that we've forgotten the context for all that language. This gave me further resolve to refine the text, define it, and give it context that was both historical and personal to Richard III, Shakespeare, and me.

Finally, I began a painstaking, word-by-word analysis and clarification in tandem with my intrepid dramaturg, the British actress Ishia Bennison. We combed through the script, reading it aloud with all her RSC cred and my Bronx-bred *coraje* and put the play together in a way in which we both understood the words, the context, and the poetry.

It was respectful and collaborative. Together we changed words, syntax, placement, and tried our best to keep the best of Shakespeare in tact without sacrificing the originality of Migdalia. Ishia, as an actress, also double-checked that the words were speakable for both American and British actors.

The stressful part, as ever, was the deadline. We had only six weeks to complete the first draft of *Richard III*, because I took him on so close to the Play On Shakespeare Festival of readings at Classic Stage Company in NYC in June 2019, wherein the entire Shakespeare canon — all translated by contemporary playwrights, directors, and dramaturgs — was to be presented. Luckily, my having already translated *Macbeth* gave me some shortcuts to the soul of *Richard*.

I hope scholars understand the uniqueness of this approach. It's not just some reductive No Fear Shakespeare. I have a specific, theatrical voice that I'm applying to this translation, which means it'll have a different kind of resonance than a literal translation or a translation from a grad student in Shakespearian studies or Shakespeare semiotics. I'm looking at these plays as a dramatist would — not a scholar. Thereby, enhancing the drama with modern language, but not detracting from it — making it present and pertinent in a way that isn't archival, dry, and academic.

Shakespeare will survive my scrutiny. My work on this play enhanced my craft as an artist, and, I believe my craft as an artist rejuvenated the work by preserving its lyricism while making the words more accessible to a modern audience. It's the 21st Century, people. Time to right the sexist, racist, and ableist wrongs of the Western Canon by viewing it through the multidimensional gaze of a modern audience and build on it or over it — into the future. And what about the future?

In this, the year 2020, which paralleled 1918, and then whisked historians back to 1665 and 1346, we again look to old stories and ancestors and new medicine and science to make sense of our world. And thus my first production of this translation came at the unlikeliest of times, during the pandemic Summer of 2020, in Sunderland, in the north of England in an outdoor production in an old churchyard with the audience masked and yearning to escape into the world that only a dramatist can provide — actors and audience breathing as one. Even when taking a breath can be dangerous, we, humans, risk it for the feeling of sharing some humanity, some laughter, some tragedy.

I think Richard and Shakespeare and I made some history this year.

We are all still alive.

Migdalia Cruz
January 2021

CAST OF CHARACTERS
(in order of speaking)

KING HENRY VI & GHOST OF HENRY VI

QUEEN MARGARET, widow of Henry VI

RICHARD, DUKE OF GLOUCESTER (later KING RICHARD III), brother of Edward IV

GEORGE, DUKE OF CLARENCE, brother of Edward IV and his GHOST

SIR ROBERT BRAKENBURY, Lieutenant of the Tower of London; Clarence's KEEPER

WILLIAM, LORD HASTINGS, Lord Chamberlain and his GHOST

LADY ANNE, Prince Edward's widow and her GHOST

ANTHONY WOODEVILLE, EARL of (Lord) RIVERS, Queen Elizabeth's brother and his GHOST

MARQUIS OF (Lord) DORSET, Queen Elizabeth's son from a previous marriage

QUEEN ELIZABETH, wife of Edward IV

DUKE OF BUCKINGHAM, follower of Richard, Duke of Gloucester and his GHOST

LORD STANLEY, the Earl of Derby

SIR WILLIAM CATESBY, follower of Richard, Duke of Gloucester

TWO MURDERERS, follower of Richard, Duke of Gloucester

KING EDWARD IV

DUCHESS OF YORK, mother of Edward IV, Clarence, Richard III

THREE CITIZENS

RICHARD, DUKE OF YORK, son of Edward IV and his GHOST

MESSENGER

EDWARD, PRINCE OF WALES, (later Edward V), son of Edward IV and his GHOST

CAST OF CHARACTERS

LORD MAYOR OF LONDON

CARDINAL BOURCHIER, Archbishop of Canterbury

SIR RICHARD RATCLIFFE, follower of Richard, Duke of Gloucester

BISHOP OF ELY

SCRIVENER

PAGE

SIR JAMES TYRREL, follower of Richard, Duke of Gloucester

MESSENGERS 1, 2, 3

SHERIFF

HENRY, EARL OF RICHMOND (later Henry VII, son-in-law to Lord Stanley)

DUKE OF NORFOLK, follower of Richard, Duke of Gloucester

SIR JAMES BLUNT, follower of Richmond

EARL OF OXFORD/LORD, follower of Richmond

LORD GREY, Queen Elizabeth's son from a previous marriage and his GHOST (non-speaking role)

SIR THOMAS VAUGHAN and his GHOST (non-speaking role)

Other Guards, Gentlemen, Citizens, Nobles, Soldiers

Pronunciation Guide:

Bretagne=BREHT-tahn
Catesby=KAYTS-bee
Derby=DAHR-bee
Ely=EE-lee
Gloucester=GLAHS-ter
Hereford=HER-ferd
Jesu=Jay-soo
Leicester=LEHS-ter

Lethe=LEE-thee
Norfolk=NAWR-fuhk
Salisbury=SAWLZ-bree
Tewkesbury=CHOUKS-bree
Tyrrel=TI-ruhl
Warwick=WAW-rik
Zounds=ZOONS

PROLOGUE

(From things said about Richard in HENRY VI, Part 3)

From the shadows, we hear voices from Richard's past. He hears
them. He always hears them, but then He just plays his music louder.
The song at the top is "London Calling" by the Clash. Richard is
either lead on this song or just listening.

ALL THE WOMEN

   "O, Jesus bless us, he is born with teeth!"

QUEEN MARGARET

   But thou art … a foul mis-shapen stigmatic,

KING HENRY VI

   … "Good Gloucester" and "good devil" were alike,

QUEEN MARGARET

   … Mark'd by your mother's womb to be avoided,

KING HENRY VI

   … rue the hour that ever thou was born. 5

   The owl shrieked at thy birth, — an evil sign …

QUEEN MARGARET

   As venomous toads, or lizards' dread stings.

KING HENRY VI

   The night-crow cries call forth a luckless time;

   Dogs howl, and hideous tempests shake down trees;

QUEEN MARGARET

   Ay, thou was born to be a plague to men. 10

KING HENRY VI

   Thy mother felt more than a mother's pain,

   Brought forth an indigested and deformed lump,

ALL THE WOMEN

   'O, Jesus bless us, he is born with teeth!'

1

KING HENRY VI

To signify thou came to bite the world:

QUEEN MARGARET

Where is that devil's butcher — 15

GLOUCESTER/RICHARD

— I have no brother, I am like no brother.

*Over the recording of The Clash's, "London Calling," and over the
sound of dogs snarling, owls hooting, people dying, we see Richard of
Gloucester enter and wash his short sword in a horses' trough. The
water runs red and swirls at his feet. He mounts his sword upon a
wall. Then thinks better of it, takes it down and puts it back into its
sheath at his belt. The sounds go silent. Then he speaks.*

ACT 1 ◆ SCENE 1

OUTSIDE THE TOWER OF LONDON

Enter Richard, Duke of Gloucester, alone. He addresses the audience

RICHARD

Now is the winter of our discontent
Made glorious summer by this son of York,
And all the clouds that glowered upon our house
Buried in the deep bosom of the ocean.
Now are our brows bound with victorious wreaths, 5
Our bloodied arms hung up for monuments,
Our stern alarms changed to merry meetings,
Our dreadful marches to delightful melodies.
Grim-faced war has smoothed his wrinkled brow;
And now, instead of mounting armoured steeds 10
To fright the souls of fearful adversaries,
He capers nimbly in a lady's chamber
To the lascivious pleasing of a lute.
But I, that am not shaped for sportive tricks
Nor made to court an amorous looking glass; 15

2

I, that am crudely shaped, and lack love's majesty
To strut before a wanton ambling nymph;
I, that am curtailed of this fair proportion,
Cheated of feature by dissembling Nature
Deformed, unfinished, sent before my time   20
Into this mortal world, scarce half made up,
And still so lame and unfashionable
That dogs bark at me as I limp by them —
Why, I, in this pastoral time of peace,
Have no delight to pass away the time,   25
Unless to see my shadow in the sun
And sing above my own deformity.
And therefore, since I cannot prove a lover
To while away these fair well-spoken days,
I am determined to prove a villain   30
And hate the idle pleasures of these days.
Plots have I laid, dangerous first steps taken,
With drunken prophecies, false words, and dreams
To set my brother Clarence and the king
In deadly hate, the one against the other;   35
And if King Edward be as true and just
As I am subtle, false and treacherous,
This day should Clarence closely be caged up
About a prophecy which says that 'G'
Of Edward's heirs the murderer shall be.   40
Dive, thoughts, down to my soul; here Clarence comes.
        Enter Clarence, surrounded by guards, and Brakenbury
(to George of Clarence, his elder brother)
Brother, good day. What means this armed guard
That waits upon your grace?
CLARENCE
His majesty,

Tending to my person's safety, appointed   45
This escort to convey me to the Tower.

RICHARD

Upon what cause?

CLARENCE

Because my name is George.

RICHARD

Oh, no, my lord, that fault is none of yours;
He should for that condemn your godfathers.   50
But what's the matter, Clarence, may I know?

CLARENCE

Yea, Richard, when I know; but I protest
As yet I do not. But, as I can learn,
He follows such mad prophecies and dreams,
And says a wizard told him that by "G"   55
His off-spring disinherited should be.
And for my name of George begins with G,
It follows in his thought that I am he,
Has moved his highness to imprison me.

RICHARD

Why, this it is, when men are ruled by women: 60
'Tis not the King that sends you to the Tower;
Elizabeth — his wife, Clarence, 'tis she
That tempts him to this harsh extremity.
Was it not she and that good man of honour,
The Lord Rivers, her pious brother there,   65
That made him send Lord Hastings to the Tower,
From where this present day he is delivered?
We are not safe, Clarence; we are not safe.

CLARENCE

By heaven, I think there is no man secure
But the queen's kindred and secret couriers   70

RICHARD

    I'll tell you what: I think 'tis for the best,

    If we will keep in favor with the King,

    Beware the Queen and wear her livery.

BRAKENBURY

    I beseech your graces both to pardon me.

    His majesty has strictly commanded   75

    That no man shall have private conference,

    To whatsoever degree, with your brother.

RICHARD

    Even so; if it please your worship, Brakenbury,

    You may partake of anything we say.

    We speak no treason, man; we say the King   80

    Is wise and virtuous, and his noble Queen

    Well served in years, fair, and not jealous.

    And that the queen's kindred are made gentlefolks.

    How say you, sir? Can you deny all this?

BRAKENBURY

    With this, my lord, I have nought to do.   85

    I do beseech your grace to pardon me, and also

    Refrain from conversing with the noble duke.

CLARENCE

    We know thy orders Brakenbury, and will obey.

RICHARD

    We are the queen's "abjects," and must obey.

    Brother, farewell. I will go to the king,   90

    And do whatever you will need me to do,

    That I need to in order to free you.

    Meantime, our deep disgrace in brotherhood

    Touches me deeper than you can imagine.

CLARENCE

    I know it please not either of us well.   95

RICHARD

Well, your imprisonment shall not be … long;

I will release you, or else lie down for you.

Meantime have patience.

CLARENCE

No choice. I must. Farewell.

Exit Clarence, Brakenbury, and Guard

RICHARD

Go, tread the path that thou shalt ne'er return; 100

Simple, plain Clarence, I do love thee so

That I will shortly send thy soul to heaven,

If heaven will take the present from my hands.

But who comes here? The now-freed Lord Hastings?

Enter Lord Hastings

HASTINGS

Good time of day unto my gracious lord. 105

RICHARD

As much unto my good Lord Chamberlain.

Well are you welcome to this open air.

How has your lordship braved imprisonment?

HASTINGS

With patience, noble lord, as prisoners must;

But I shall live, my lord, to give them thanks

That were the cause of my imprisonment. 110

RICHARD

No doubt, no doubt; and so shall Clarence too,

For they that were your enemies are his

And have prevailed as much on him as you.

HASTINGS

More pity noble eagles should be caged,

When lowly kites and buzzards fly freely. 115

What news abroad?

RICHARD

No news so bad abroad as this at home:

The King is sickly, weak, and melancholy,

His physicians fear for him mightily.

HASTINGS

Now by Saint John, that news is bad indeed!   120

O, he has long kept unhealthy habits,

And over-much consumed his royal person.

Where is he, in his bed?

RICHARD

He is.

Go you before, and I will follow you.   125

Exit Hastings

He cannot live, I hope, and must not die

Till George be saddled on swift horse up to heaven.

Which done, God take King Edward with his mercy,

And leave the world for me to bustle in.

For then, I'll marry Warwick's youngest daughter   130

Though I did kill her husband and his father.

(pause)

The readiest way to make the wench amends

Is to become her husband and her father;

But yet I run before my horse to market:

Clarence still breathes; Edward still lives and reigns.   135

But once they're gone, then must I count my gains.

Exit

ACT 1 ◆ SCENE 2
NEAR THE TOWER OF LONDON

Lady Anne enters with the corpse of her father-in-law
Henry the Sixth. Men with Halberds {weapons with points like
spears and battle-axe handles} guard it. Lady Anne is attended
by other Gentlemen.

ANNE

    Set down, set down your honourable load,
    If honor may be shrouded in a hearse,
    While I awhile devoutly mourn and lament
    Th' untimely fall of virtuous Lancaster.
    Poor key-cold figure, of our king Henry,   5
    Pale ashes of the house of Lancaster,
    Thou bloodless remnant of that royal blood,
    Be it lawful that I thus call forth thy ghost
    To hear the lamentations of poor Anne,
    Wife to thy Edward, to thy slaughtered son,   10
    Stabbed by the selfsame hand that made these wounds.
    Lo, through these portals that poured forth thy life
    I pour the tearful balm of my poor eyes.
    O, cursèd be the hand that made these holes;
    Cursèd the blood that let your blood spill hence.   15
    Cursèd the heart that had the heart to do it.
    If ever he have wife, let her be made
    More miserable by the death of him
    Than I am made by my young lord and thee.
    — Come now towards Chertsey with your holy load,   20
    Taken from St. Paul's to be buried there.

Enter Richard, Duke of Gloucester.

RICHARD

    Stay, you that bear the corpse, and set it down.

ANNE

What black magician conjures up this fiend
To stop devoted charitable deeds?

RICHARD

Villains, set down the corpse, or, by Saint Paul,   25
I'll make a corpse of him that disobeys.

They put down the corpse which rests on a wooden bier.

ANNE

What, do you tremble? Are you all afraid?
Oh, no, I blame you not, for you are mortal,
And mortal eyes cannot endure the devil.
— Begone, thou dreadful minister of hell!   30
Thou wields but power over his mortal body;
His soul thou cannot have. Therefore begone.

RICHARD

Sweet saint, for charity, be not so curst.

ANNE

Foul devil, for God's sake go, and trouble us not,
For thou has made the happy earth thy hell,   35
Filled it with cursing cries and deep exclaims.
If thou delight to view thy heinous deeds,
Behold this pattern of thy butcheries.
— O gentlemen, see, see dead Henry's wounds
Open their congealed mouths and bleed afresh.   40
— Blush, blush, thou lump of foul deformity,
For 'tis thy presence that exhales this blood
From cold and empty veins where no blood dwells.
Thy deeds, inhuman and unnatural,
Provoke this deluge supernatural.   45

(Anne touches the blood suddenly dripping off the corpse)

As earth does swallow up this good king's blood,
Which his hell-governed arm has butchered.

RICHARD

    Lady, you know no rules of charity,

    Which renders good for bad, blessings for curses.

ANNE

    Villain, thou knows not law of God nor man.   50

    Fierce beasts even know some touch of pity.

RICHARD

    But I know none, and therefore am no beast.

ANNE

    Oh wonderful, when devils tell the truth!

RICHARD

    More wonderful, when angels are so angry.

    Grant me, divine perfection of a woman,   55

    For these supposèd crimes to give me leave

    By circumstance but to acquit myself.

ANNE

    Grant me, disordered infection of a man,

    For these known evils, to but give me leave

    By circumstance, to curse thy cursèd self.   60

RICHARD

    Fairer than tongue can name thee, let me have

    With patience, some chance to excuse myself.

ANNE

    Fouler than heart can think thee, thou can make

    No honest excuse but to hang thyself.

RICHARD

    By such despair I should accuse myself.   65

ANNE

    And by despairing shalt thou stand excused

    For doing worthy vengeance on thyself

    That did unworthy slaughter upon others.

RICHARD

Say that I slew them not.

ANNE

Then say they were not slain.   70

But dead they are, and, devilish slave, by thee.

RICHARD

I did not kill your husband.

ANNE

Why, then he is alive.

RICHARD

Nay, he is dead, and slain by Edward's hands.

ANNE

In thy foul throat thou lies, God grant me.   75

Did thou not kill this king?

RICHARD

I'll grant you that.

ANNE

Does grant me, hedgehog? Then God grant me too

Thou may be damnèd for that wicked deed.

O, he was gentle, mild and virtuous.   80

RICHARD

The better for the King of Heaven that has him.

ANNE

He is in heaven, where thou shalt never go.

RICHARD

Let him thank me that helped to send him there,

For he was fitter for that place than earth.

ANNE

And thou unfit for any place but hell.   85

RICHARD

Yes, one place else, if you will hear me name it.

ANNE

Some dungeon.

RICHARD

Your bedchamber.

ANNE

Ill rest befall the chamber where thou lies.

RICHARD

So will it, madam, till I lie with you.   90

ANNE

I hope so.

RICHARD

I know so. But, gentle Lady Anne,

To leave this keen encounter of our wits

And so follow reason's slower method:

Is not the causer of the ill-timed deaths   95

Of these Plantagenets, Henry and Edward,

As guilty as the executioner?

ANNE

Thou was the cause, and most accursed effect.

RICHARD

Your beauty was the cause of that effect:

Your beauty, that did haunt me in my sleep   100

To undertake the death of all the world,

So I might live one hour in your sweet bosom.

ANNE

If I thought that, I tell thee, homicide,

These nails should rend that beauty from my cheeks.

RICHARD

These eyes could not endure that beauty's wreck;   105

You should not blemish it, if I stood by.

As all the world is cheerèd by the sun,

So I by that. It is my day, my life.

ANNE

Black night o'ershade thy day, and death thy life.

RICHARD

Curse not thyself, fair creature; thou art both. 110

ANNE

I would I were, to be revenged on thee.

RICHARD

It is a quarrel most unnatural,

To be revenged on him that loves thee.

ANNE

It is a quarrel just and reasonable,

To be revenged on him that killed my husband. 115

RICHARD

He that bereft thee, lady, of thy husband,

Did it to help thee to a better husband.

ANNE

His better does not breathe upon the earth.

RICHARD

He lives that loves thee better than he could.

ANNE

Name him. 120

RICHARD

Plantagenet.

ANNE

Why, that was he.

RICHARD

The selfsame name, but one of better nature.

ANNE

Where is he?

RICHARD

Here 125

(she spits at him)

Why does thou spit at me?

ANNE

Would it were mortal poison, for thy sake.

Out of my sight! Thou does infect mine eyes.

RICHARD

Thine eyes, sweet lady, have infected mine.

ANNE

Would they were basilisks to strike thee dead,   130

With serpent stares that kill with a grim glance.

RICHARD

I would they were, that I might die at once;

For now they kill me with a living death.

Those eyes of thine from mine have drawn salt tears,

Shamed their aspects with store of childish drops;   135

These eyes, which never shed remorseful tear —

Thy beauty has made them blind with weeping.

I never begged friend, nor enemy;

My tongue could never learn sweet smoothing word.

But now thy beauty is offered as fee,   140

My proud heart begs, and prompts my tongue to speak.

(she looks scornfully at him)

Teach not thy lip such scorn, for it was made

For kissing, lady, not for such contempt.

If thy revengeful heart cannot forgive,

Lo, here I lend thee this sharp-pointed sword,   145

Which if thou please to hide in this true breast

And let the soul forth that adores thee,

I lay it naked to the deadly stroke

And humbly beg the death upon my knee.

(he kneels, opens his shirt showing his chest. She aims at it with his sword)

Nay, do not pause, for I did kill King Henry,   150

But 'twas thy beauty that provoked me.

14

Nay, now quickly; 'twas I that stabbed young Edward,

But 'twas thy heavenly face that set me on.

(she lets the sword fall)

Take up the sword again, or take up me.

ANNE

Arise, thou, liar; though I wish thy death,   155

I will not be thy executioner.

RICHARD

Then bid me kill myself, and I will do it.

ANNE

I have already.

RICHARD

That was in thy rage.

Speak it again and, even with the word,   160

This hand, which for thy love did kill thy love,

Shall for thy love kill a far truer love;

To both their deaths shalt thou be accessory.

ANNE

I would I knew thy heart.

RICHARD

'Tis figured in my tongue.   165

ANNE

I fear me both are false.

RICHARD

Then never man was true.

ANNE

Well, well, put up your sword.

RICHARD

Say then my peace is made.

ANNE

That shalt thou know hereafter.   170

RICHARD

But shall I live in hope?

ANNE

All men I hope live so.

RICHARD

So swear to wear this ring.

ANNE

To take is not to give.

RICHARD

Look how my ring encompasses thy finger;   175

Just as thy breast encloses my poor heart.

Wear both of them, for both of them are thine.

And if thy poor devoted servant may

But beg one favor at thy gracious hand,

Thou does confirm his happiness forever.   180

ANNE

What is it?

RICHARD

That it may please you leave these sad designs

To him that has most cause to be a mourner,

And presently repair to Crosby House,

Where, after I have solemnly interred   185

At Chertsey Monastery this noble king

And wet his grave with my repentant tears,

I will with all expedient duty see you.

Grant me this wish.

ANNE

With all my heart, and much it joys me too   190

To see you are become so penitent.

RICHARD

Bid me farewell.

ANNE

'Tis more than you deserve;

But since you teach me how to flatter you,

Imagine I have said farewell already.   195

Exit Anne

GENTLEMAN

Towards Chertsey, noble lord?

RICHARD

No, only Whitefriars; attend my coming.

Exit the rest with the corpse

Was ever woman in this humour wooed?

Was ever woman in this humour won?

I'll have her, but I will not keep her long.   200

What? I that killed her husband and his father,

To take her in her heart's extremest hate,

With curses in her mouth, tears in her eyes,

Bleeding witness of my hatred nearby,

Having God, her conscience and these strikes against me,   205

And I no friends to back my suit besides

But all those plain devil and dark-disguised looks?

And yet to win her?!

All the world 'gainst me, nothing for me! Ha!

Has she forgot already that brave prince,   210

Edward, her lord, whom I, some three months since,

Stabbed in my angry mood at Tewkesbury?

A sweeter and a lovelier gentleman,

Framed with the great bountiful gifts of nature,

Young, valiant, wise and, no doubt, right royal,   215

The spacious world cannot again afford;

And will she yet lower her eyes on me,

That cropped the golden prime of this sweet prince

And made her widow to a woeful bed?

On me, whose all does not equal Edward's half? 220
On me, that limps and am misshapen thus?
My dukedom is but a small worthless sum,
I do mistake my person all this while!
Upon my life, she finds, although I cannot,
Myself to be a marvelous proper man. 225
I'll pay a ransom for a looking-glass
And so employ a score or two of tailors
To study fashions to adorn my body;
But first I'll toss yon fellow in his grave,
And then return lamenting to my love. 230
Shine out, fair sun, till I've a lookingglass
That I may see my shadow as I pass.

Exit

ACT 1 ◆ SCENE 3

LONDON: A ROOM IN KING EDWARD IV'S PALACE

Enter Queen Elizabeth, Lord Rivers, and Lord Dorset

RIVERS

Have patience, madam. There's no doubt his majesty
Will soon recover his accustomed health.

DORSET

If you take it badly, it makes him worse;
Therefore for God's sake entertain good comfort
And cheer his grace with quick and merry eyes. 5

QUEEN ELIZABETH

If he were dead, what would become of me?

RIVERS

No other harm but loss of such a lord.

QUEEN ELIZABETH

The loss of such a lord includes all harms.

RIVERS

    The heavens have blessed you with a goodly son

    To be your comforter when he is gone.   10

QUEEN ELIZABETH

    Ah, he is young, and his future kingship

    Is put unto the trust of Richard Gloucester,

    A man that loves not me, nor none of you.

RIVERS

    Is it concluded he shall be Protector?

QUEEN ELIZABETH

    It is determined, not concluded yet;   15

    But so it must be, if the King should perish.

                Enter Buckingham and Stanley Earl of Derby

DORSET

    Here come the Lords Buckingham and Stanley.

BUCKINGHAM

    Good time of day unto your royal grace.

STANLEY

    God make your majesty joyful, as you have been.

QUEEN ELIZABETH

    Saw you the King today, my Lord Stanley?   20

STANLEY

    Only now the Duke of Buckingham and I

    Are come from visiting his majesty.

QUEEN ELIZABETH

    How likely is his recovery, lords?

BUCKINGHAM

    Madam, good hope. His grace speaks cheerfully.

QUEEN ELIZABETH

    God grant him health. Did you confer with him?   25

BUCKINGHAM

    Ay, madam; he desires to repair the rift

Between the Duke of Gloucester and your brothers,
And between them and my Lord Chamberlain,
And summoned them to his royal presence.

QUEEN ELIZABETH

Would all were well, but that will never be;   30
I fear our happiness is at its height.

Enter Richard and Hastings

RICHARD

They do me wrong, and I will not endure it!
Who is it that complains unto the King
That I indeed am stern and love them not?
By Saintly Paul, they but lightly love his grace   35
That fill his ears with such contentious rumors.
Because I cannot flatter, and look fair,
Smile in men's faces, fawn, deceive and cheat,
Nod like fake French followers seeking favor,
I must be held a poisonous enemy.   40
Cannot a plain man live and think no harm,
Without his simple truth being abused
By silk-tongued, sly, and prattling louts?

DORSET

And to whom in your presence speaks your grace?

RICHARD

To thee, that has not honesty nor grace.   45
When have I injured thee? When done thee wrong?
— Or thee? — Or thee? — Or any of your faction?
A plague upon you all! His royal grace,
Whom God preserve better than you would wish,
Cannot be left in peace for even a breath   50
Without your troubling him with lewd complaints.

QUEEN ELIZABETH

Brother in-law, you mistake the matter.

20

RICHARD

    I cannot tell; the world is grown so bad

    That wee wrens take prey where eagles dare not perch.   55

    Since every lout became a gentleman,

    There's many a gentle person made a lout.

QUEEN ELIZABETH

    Come, come, we know your meaning, brother Gloucester.

    You envy my rise and that of my friends,

    God grant we may never have need of you.   60

RICHARD

    Meantime, God grants that I have need of you.

    Our brother is imprisoned by your means,

    Myself disgraced, and the nobility

    Held in contempt, while great promotions

    Are daily given to mark as lords those   65

    That scarce some two days since were worth a mark.

QUEEN ELIZABETH

    By God that raised me to this lofty height

    From that contented life which I enjoyed,

    I never did incense his majesty

    Against the Duke of Clarence, but have been   70

    An earnest advocate to plead for him.

    My lord, you do me shameful injury

    Painting me with false and vile suspicions.

RICHARD

    You may deny that you were the reason

    For my Lord Hastings' sad imprisonment.   75

RIVERS

    She may, my lord, for —

RICHARD

    She may, Lord Rivers; why, who knows not so?

    She may do more, sir, than denying that:

She may help you to many fair preferments,
And then deny her aiding hand therein 80
And say those honors are highly deserved
What may she not? She may, Holy Mary, may she.

RIVERS

What, marry, may she?

RICHARD

What, marry, may she? Marry with a king,

QUEEN ELIZABETH

My Lord of Gloucester, I have too long borne 85
Your blunt rebukes and your bitter scoffs.
By heaven, I will acquaint his majesty
Of those gross taunts that oft I have endured.
I had rather be a country servant maid
Than a great queen that suffers such treatment, 90
To be so baited, scorned, and stormed at.

Enter Queen Margaret, unseen by the others

Small joy have I in being England's queen.

QUEEN MARGARET *(aside)*

Less than nothing be that small, God beseech you.
Thy honour, state and throne is due to me.

RICHARD

What? Threaten me with telling to the king? 95
Tell him, and spare not. Look what I have said
I will vouch for it in the king's presence.
I dare take the risk to be sent to th' Tower.
'Tis time to speak; my efforts quite forgot.

QUEEN MARGARET *(aside)*

Out, devil! I do remember them too well: 100
Thou kill'dst my husband Henry in the Tower,
And Edward, my poor son, at Tewkesbury.

22

RICHARD

    While you were queen, ay, or your husband king,

    I was a packhorse in his great affairs,

    A weeder-out of his proud adversaries,   105

    A liberal rewarder of his friends.

    To royalize his blood, I spent mine own.

QUEEN MARGARET *(aside)*

    Ay, and much better thy blood than his.

RICHARD

    In all which time, you and your first husband

    Stood steadfast with the House of Lancaster.   110

    — And Rivers, so were you. — Was not your husband

    In Margaret's battle at St. Albans slain?

    — Let me put in your minds, lest you forget,

    What you once were, and what you now are;

    Unlike, what I have been, and what I am.   115

QUEEN MARGARET *(aside)*

    A murderous villain, and so still thou art.

RICHARD

    Poor Clarence forsook his bride's father Warwick,

    Ay, and forswore his oath — may Jesus pardon —

QUEEN MARGARET *(aside)*

    May God revenge.

RICHARD

    To fight on Edward's party for the crown,   120

    And for his payment poor lord, he's locked up.

    I wish to God my heart were flint, like Edward's,

    Or Edward's soft and pitiful, like mine.

    I am too childish-foolish for this world.

QUEEN MARGARET *(aside)*

    Hasten to hell for shame, and leave this world,   125

    Thou cacodemon. There thy kingdom is.

RIVERS

My Lord of Gloucester, in those warring days

Which here you use to prove us enemies,

We followed then our lord, our sovereign king.

So should we you, if you should be our king.   130

RICHARD

If I should be? I had rather be a peddlar.

Far be it from my heart, the thought thereof.

QUEEN ELIZABETH

As little joy, my lord, as you suppose

You should enjoy, were you this country's king,   135

Same little joy you may suppose in me

That I enjoy, being the queen thereof.

QUEEN MARGARET *(aside)*

As little joy enjoys the queen thereof,

For I am she, and altogether joyless.

I can no longer hold back my tongue.   140

(comes forward from the shadows)

Hear me, you wrangling pirates, that now fight

To share that which you have pilfered from me:

Which of you trembles not, that looks on me?

When I was queen, you bowed like subjects,

Now that you deposed me, you quake like rebels.   145

— Ah, noble villain, do not turn away.

RICHARD

Ah, Queen Margaret, foul wrinkled witch, what conjured thou

before me?

QUEEN MARGARET

But a litany of what thou hast marred;

That will I make before I let thee go.

RICHARD

Wert thou not banished on pain of death?   150

QUEEN MARGARET

    I was, but I do find more pain in banishment

    Than death can yield me here by my abode.

    A husband and a son thou ow'st to me;

    — And thou a kingdom; — all of you, allegiance.

    This sorrow that I have, by right is yours,   155

    And all the pleasures you usurp are mine.

RICHARD

    The curse my noble father laid on thee

    When thou mocked his warlike brows with paper crown,

    And with thy scorn drew rivers from his eyes,

    And then handed him to dry them, a cloak   160

    Steeped in my brother Rutland's blameless blood.

    Our father's curses then, from bitter loss

    Pronounced against thee, now are fall'n upon thee;

    And God, not we, has plagued thy bloody deed.

QUEEN ELIZABETH

    So just is God, to right the innocent.   165

HASTINGS

    Oh, 'twas the foulest deed to slay that babe,

    And the most merciless, that e'er was heard of.

RIVERS

    Tyrants themselves wept when it was reported.

DORSET

    No man but prophesied revenge for it.

BUCKINGHAM

    Northumberland, then present, wept to see it.   170

QUEEN MARGARET

    What? Were you all snarling before I came,

    Ready to catch each other by the throat,

    And turn you all your hatred now on me?

    Did York's dread curse prevail so much with heaven

That Henry's death, my lovely Edward's death, 175
Their kingdom's loss, my woeful banishment,
Should all but answer for that foolish brat, Rutland?
Can curses pierce the clouds and enter heaven?
Why then give way, dull clouds, to my quick curses.
Though not by war, by excess die your king, 180
As ours by murder, to make him a king.
— Edward thy son, that now is Prince of Wales,
For Edward our son, that was Prince of Wales,
Die in his youth, by same untimely violence.
Thyself a queen, for me that was a queen, 185
Outlive thy glory, like my wretched self.
Long mayst thou live to wail thy children's death
And see another, as I see thee now,
Decked in thy rights as thou art placed in mine.
Die neither mother, wife, nor England's queen. 190
— Rivers and Dorset, you were standers-by,
And so wast thou, Lord Hastings, when my son
Was stabbed with bloody daggers. God, I pray,
That none of you may live his natural age,
But are by some vile accident cut off. 195

RICHARD

Have done thy charm, thou hateful withered hag.

QUEEN MARGARET

And leave thee out? Stay, dog, for thou shalt hear me.
If heaven have any grievous plague in store
Exceeding those that I can wish upon thee,
O, let them keep it till thy sins be ripe, 200
And then hurl down their indignation
On thee, the troubler of the poor world's peace.
The worm of conscience still gnaw at thy soul;
Let no sleep close that deadly eye of thine,

Unless it be while some tormenting dream 205
Frightens thee with a hell of ugly devils.
Thou elvish-marked, abortive, rooting hog,
Thou that wast branded by thy monstrous birth
The slave of nature and the son of hell;
Thou slander of thy heavy mother's womb, 210
Thou loathsome issue of thy father's loins,
Thou rag of honor, thou detested —

RICHARD
Margaret.

QUEEN MARGARET
Richard!

RICHARD
Ha? 215

QUEEN MARGARET
I call thee not.

RICHARD
I cry for mercy then, for I did think
That you had called me all those bitter names.

QUEEN MARGARET
Why, so I did, but looked for no reply.
O, let me place a period on my curse. 220

RICHARD
'Tis done by me and ends in "Margaret."

QUEEN ELIZABETH
Thus have you breathed your curse against yourself.

QUEEN MARGARET
Poor painted queen, fake flourish of my fortune,
Why strew'st thou sugar on that swollen spider,
Whose deadly web ensnareth thee in lies? 225
Fool, fool, thou hones a knife to kill thyself.
The day will come that thou shalt wish for me

To help thee curse that poisonous hunch-backed toad.

HASTINGS

False-boding woman, end thy frantic curse,

Lest you tempt harm by trying our patience.   230

DORSET

Dispute not with her; she's a lunatic.

QUEEN MARGARET

Peace, master Dorset! So impudent!

BUCKINGHAM

Peace, peace, for shame, if not for charity.

QUEEN MARGARET

Urge neither charity nor shame on me.

(to the others)

Uncharitably with me have you dealt,   235

And shamefully my hopes by you are butchered.

My charity is outrage, life my shame,

And in that shame, still lives my sorrow's rage.

BUCKINGHAM

Have done, have done.

QUEEN MARGARET

O princely Buckingham, I'll kiss thy hand   240

In allegiance and amity with thee.

Fortune befall thee and thy noble house.

Thy garments are not spotted with our blood,

Nor thou within the compass of my curse.

O Buckingham, take heed of yonder dog.   245

Look when he fawns, he bites; and when he bites,

His venom teeth will fester to the death.

Have naught to do with him, beware of him;

RICHARD

What does she say, my Lord of Buckingham?

BUCKINGHAM

Nothing that I respect, my gracious lord.   250

QUEEN MARGARET

So, dost thou scorn me for my gentle counsel,

And soothe the devil that I warn thee from?

O, but remember this another day,

When he shall split thy very heart with sorrow,

And say poor Margaret was a prophetess.   255

— Live each of you, the subjects of his hate,

And he to yours, and all of you to God's.

Queen Margaret exits

BUCKINGHAM

My hair does stand on end to hear her curses.

RIVERS

And so does mine. Why does she wander freely?

RICHARD

I cannot blame her; by God's holy Mother,   260

She has had too much wrong, and I repent

My part in all that I have done to her.

QUEEN ELIZABETH

I never did her any to my knowledge.

RICHARD

Yet you have all the advantage she's lost.

Indeed, as for Clarence, he is well repaid: 265

He is penned like a porker for his pains.

God pardon them that are the cause thereof.

RIVERS

A virtuous and a Christian-like conclusion,

To pray for them that have done harm to us.

RICHARD *(aside)*

Had I prayed now I'd have damned myself.   270

Enter Catesby

CATESBY

Madam, his majesty does call for you,

— And for your grace, — and yours, my gracious lords.

QUEEN ELIZABETH

Catesby, I come. — Lords, will you go with me?

RIVERS

We wait upon your grace.

Exit all but Richard, Duke of Gloucester

RICHARD

I do the mischief, and now begin to brawl.   275

The secret wrongs that I set afoot

I lay blame unto the faultless others.

I do weep for so many simple fools:

Clarence, who I indeed have cast in darkness,

Also for Stanley, Hastings, Buckingham,   280

And tell them 'tis the Queen and her allies

That stir the King against the Duke my brother.

Now they believe it, and thereby thrust me

Into revenge on her brother and sons.

But then I sigh, and, with a piece of Scripture,   285

Tell them that God bids us do good for evil;

And thus I clothe my naked villainy

With odd old ends, stol'n forth from Holy Words

And seem a saint when most I play the devil.

Enter two Murderers

But soft, here come my executioners.   290

— How now, my hardy, stout, resolvéd mates;

Are you now going to dispatch this thing?

FIRST MURDERER

We are, my lord, and come to fetch the warrant,

That we may be admitted where he is.

RICHARD

Very good thinking. I have it on my person.   295

But sirs, be sudden in the execution,

Therefore keep steadfast; do not hear him plead,

For Clarence is well-spoken and perhaps

May move your hearts to pity, if you heed him.

SECOND MURDERER

Tut, tut, my lord, we will not stay to chat.   300

Talkers are not good doers; be assured

We go to use our hands and not our tongues.

RICHARD

Your eyes drop millstones when fools' eyes drip tears.

I like you, lads. Straight about your business.

Go, go, dispatch.   305

BOTH MURDERERS

We will, my noble lord.

They exit

ACT 1 ◆ SCENE 4

A ROOM IN THE TOWER OF LONDON

Enter Clarence and Brakenbury, Lieutenant of the Tower

BRAKENBURY

Why looks your grace so heavily today?

CLARENCE

Oh, I have passed a miserable night,

So full of fearful dreams, of ugly sights,

That, as I am a faithful Christian man,

I would not spend another such a night   5

Even to buy a world of happy days,

So full of dismal terror was the time.

BRAKENBURY

What was your dream, my lord? Tell me, I pray you.

CLARENCE

    It seemed that I had escaped from the Tower,

    And was sailing across to Burgundy;   10

    And in my company my brother Gloucester,

    Who from my cabin tempted me to walk

    Upon the ship's deck. There we looked toward England,

    And recalled a thousand trying times,

    During the wars of York and Lancaster,   15

    That had befall'n us. As we paced along

    Upon the dizzying planks of the deck,

    I thought that Gloucester stumbled, and in falling

    Pushed me overboard — when I thought to save him —

    Into the tumbling billows of the sea.   20

    O Lord, I thought what pain it was to drown,

    What dreadful noise of water in my ears,

    What sights of ugly death within my eyes.

    I thought I saw a thousand fearful wrecks,

    A thousand men that fishes gnawed upon,   25

    Wedges of gold, great anchors, heaps of pearl,

    Inestimable stones, priceless jewels,

    All scattered at the bottom of the sea.

BRAKENBURY

    Had you such leisure in the time of death

    To gaze upon these secrets of the deep?   30

CLARENCE

    I thought I had, and often did I strive

    To meet my ghost, but still the spiteful sea

    Stopped up my soul and would not set it free.

BRAKENBURY

    Did you awake in this sore agony?

CLARENCE

    No, no, my dream was lengthened after life.   35

O, then began the tempest to my soul.
I passed, I thought, the melancholy flood,
With that sour ferryman of whom poets write,
Unto the kingdom of perpetual night.
The first that there did greet my stranger-soul   40
Was my great father-in-law, renowned Warwick,
Who spoke: "How many lashes for perjury
Can this dark monarchy land on false Clarence?"
And at once he vanished. Then came wandering by
A shadow like an angel, with bright hair   45
Spattered with blood, and he shrieked with vengeance,
"Clarence is come, false, fleeting, perjured Clarence,
That stabbed me in the field by Tewkesbury.
Seize on him, furies! Take him unto torment!"
With that, I thought, a legion of foul fiends   50
Encircled me, and howled in my ears
Such hideous cries, that with the very noise
I, trembling, waked, and for forever after
Could not believe but that I was in hell,
Such terrible impression made my dream.   55

BRAKENBURY

No marvel, lord, that it frightened you;
I am afraid just from hearing you tell it.

CLARENCE

Ah, Brakenbury, I have done these things
That now give evidence against my soul
For Edward's sake; and see how he repays me.   60
— O God! If my deep prayers cannot appease Thee,
But Thou will be avenged on my misdeeds,
Pray execute Thy wrath on me alone;
O, spare my guiltless wife and my poor children.
— Keeper, I pray thee sit by me awhile;   65

My soul is heavy and I need to sleep.

BRAKENBURY

I will, my lord. God give your grace good rest.

Clarence sleeps, Brakenbury moves to his side
and observes Clarence from a distance where he cannot be heard

BRAKENBURY

Sorrow wrecks all seasons and sleeping hours.
Makes the night morning and the noontide night.
Princes have only titles for their glories,   70
An outward honour for an inward toil;
For empty honours imagined not earned
They often feel a world of restless cares,
That between the titled and the low-named
There's no difference but the outward fame.   75

Enter two Murderers

FIRST MURDERER

Ho, who's here?

BRAKENBURY

What do you want? And how came thou hither?

FIRST MURDERER

I would speak with Clarence, and I came hither on my legs.

BRAKENBURY

What, so brief?

SECOND MURDERER

'Tis better, sir, than to be tedious.   80

— Let him see our warrant, and talk no more.

Brakenbury reads

BRAKENBURY

I am in this commanded to deliver
The noble Duke of Clarence to your hands.
I will not question what is meant by this
So I share no guilt if I know not why.   85

34

There lies the duke asleep, and there the keys.

I'll to the King, and signify to him

That thus I have released to you my charge.

FIRST MURDERER

Do go, sir; that would be wise. Fare you well.

Exit Brakenbury

SECOND MURDERER

What, shall we stab him as he sleeps? 90

FIRST MURDERER

No. He'll say 'twas done by cowards when he wakes.

SECOND MURDERER

Why, he shall never wake until Holy Judgment Day.

FIRST MURDERER

Why, then he'll say we stabbed him sleeping.

SECOND MURDERER

The pressure of that word "Judgment" has bred a kind of remorse in me. 95

FIRST MURDERER

What? Art thou afraid?

SECOND MURDERER

Not to kill him, having a warrant, but to be damned for killing him, from which no warrant can defend me.

FIRST MURDERER

I thought thou were resolute.

SECOND MURDERER

So I am, to let him live. 100

FIRST MURDERER

I'll go back to the Duke of Gloucester and tell him so.

SECOND MURDERER

No, I pray thee wait a little. I hope this forgiving mood of mine will change. It might only hold me for a count from one to twenty.

FIRST MURDERER

How does thou feel thyself now?   105

SECOND MURDERER

In faith, some certain dregs of conscience are yet within me.

FIRST MURDERER

Remember our reward when the deed's done.

SECOND MURDERER

Zounds, he dies! I had forgot the reward.

FIRST MURDERER

Where's thy conscience now?

SECOND MURDERER

O, in the Duke of Gloucester's purse.   110

FIRST MURDERER

When he opens his purse to give us our reward, thy conscience flies out.

SECOND MURDERER

Come, shall we get to work?

FIRST MURDERER

Smash him on the noggin with the hilt of thy sword, and then dunk him into the barrel of wine in the next room.   115

SECOND MURDERER

O excellent scheme! And make a sopping sweet madeira cake of him.

FIRST MURDERER

Shush, he wakes.

SECOND MURDERER

Strike!

FIRST MURDERER

No, we'll reason with him.   120

CLARENCE

Where art thou, Brakenbury? Give me a cup of wine.

SECOND MURDERER

You shall have wine enough, my lord, anon.

CLARENCE

In God's name, what art thou?

FIRST MURDERER

A man, as you are.

CLARENCE

But not as I am, royal.   125

FIRST MURDERER

Nor you as we are, loyal.

CLARENCE

Thy voice is thunder, but thy looks are humble.

FIRST MURDERER

My voice is now the King's, my looks my own.

CLARENCE

How darkly, and how deadly does thou speak!

Your eyes do menace me. Why look you pale?   130

Who sent you hither? Why then do you come?

BOTH

To, to, to —

CLARENCE

To murder me?

BOTH

Ay, ay.

CLARENCE

You scarcely have the hearts to tell me so,   135

And therefore cannot have the hearts to do it.

How then, my friends, have I offended you?

FIRST MURDERER

Offended us you have not, but the King.

CLARENCE

I shall be reconciled to him again.

SECOND MURDERER

    Never, my lord; therefore prepare to die.   140

CLARENCE

    Before I'm convicted by course of law,

    To threaten me with death is most unlawful.

    The deed you undertake will damn you both.

FIRST MURDERER

    What we will do, we do upon command.

SECOND MURDERER

    And he that has commanded is our king.   145

CLARENCE

    Erroneous vassals, the great King of kings

    Has in the table of His law commanded

    That thou shalt do no murder. Will you then

    Reject God's edict, and fulfill a man's?

    Take heed, for He holds vengeance in His hand,   150

    To hurl upon those heads that break His law.

SECOND MURDERER

    And that same vengeance does He hurl on thee

    For false fidelity and murder too.

    Thou did receive the sacrament to fight

    On the side of the house of Lancaster.   155

FIRST MURDERER

    And like a traitor to the name of God

    Did break that vow, and with thy treacherous blade

    Unripped the bowels of thy sovereign's son.

SECOND MURDERER

    Whom thou was sworn to cherish and defend.

FIRST MURDERER

    How can thou urge God's dreadful law to us   160

    When thou has broke it to such dire extent?

CLARENCE

    Dear God! For whose sake did I that ill deed?

    For Edward, for my brother, for his sake.

    He sends you not to murder me for this,

    For in that sin he is as deep as I.   165

    If you do love my brothers, hate not me.

    And find my dear younger brother Gloucester,

    Who shall reward you better for my life

    Than Edward will for tidings of my death.

SECOND MURDERER

    You are deceived; your brother Gloucester hates you.   170

CLARENCE

    O no, he loves me, and he holds me dear.

    Go you to him from me.

FIRST MURDERER

    Ay, so we will.

CLARENCE

    Tell him, that when our father, Duke of York

    Blessed his three sons with his victorious arm,   175

    And charged us from his soul to love each other,

    He little thought of this divided friendship.

    Bid Gloucester think on this, and he will weep.

FIRST MURDERER

    Ay, millstones, were what he taught us to weep.

CLARENCE

    O, do not slander him, for he is kind.   180

FIRST MURDERER

    Kind as snow at harvest. Come, you deceive yourself.

    'Tis he that sends us to destroy you here.

CLARENCE

    It cannot be, he wept for my misfortune,

    And hugged me in his arms, and swore with sobs

That he would labour toward my release.   185
FIRST MURDERER
    Why, so he does, when he releases you
    From earthly prison to the joys of heaven.
SECOND MURDERER
    Make peace with God, for you must die, my lord.
CLARENCE
    Have you that holy feeling in your souls
    To counsel me to make my peace with God,   190
    And are you yet so blind to your own souls
    That you will war with God by murdering me?
    O sirs, consider: they that urged you on
    To do this deed will hate you for the deed.
SECOND MURDERER
    What shall we do?   195
CLARENCE
    Relent, and save your souls.
FIRST MURDERER
    Relent? No. 'Tis cowardly and womanish.
CLARENCE
    Not to relent is beastly, savage, devilish.
(to Second Murderer)
    My friend, I spy some pity in thy looks.
    O, if thine eye does not show false mercy,   200
    Come thou onto my side, and plead for my life;
    A begging prince, whom beggars pity not.
SECOND MURDERER
    Look behind you, my lord.
FIRST MURDERER
    Take that! and that!
                            Stabs him
    If all this will not do,   205

I'll drown you in the wine barrel yonder.

Exits with Clarence's body

SECOND MURDERER

A bloody deed, and desperately dispatched.

Like Pontius Pilate, I'd well wash my hands

Of this unholy murder.

Enter First Murderer

FIRST MURDERER

So now?   210

What do you mean by not helping me?

By heavens, the Duke shall know how slack you have been.

SECOND MURDERER

I wish he knew that I had saved his brother.

Take thou the fee, and tell him what I say,

For I must repent that the Duke is slain.   215

Exit Second Murderer

FIRST MURDERER

Well I will not. Go, coward as thou art.

So, I'll go hide the body in some hole

Until the duke give order for his burial.

When I have my money, I will away,

For this will come out, then I must not stay.   220

Exit First Murderer

ACT 2 ♦ SCENE 1

A ROOM IN KING EDWARD IV'S PALACE. FLOURISH

Enter an ailing King Edward, with Queen Elizabeth, Lord Dorset,
Rivers, Hastings, Catesby, Buckingham.

KING EDWARD

Noblemen, Now here is a good day's work.

You lords, continue this united league.

I every day expect a holy message

From my Redeemer to redeem me hence,

And more in peace shall my soul part to heaven,   5

Since I have made my friends at peace on earth.

— Hastings and Rivers, take each other's hand;

Disguise not your hatred, but Swear your love.

RIVERS

By heaven, my soul is purged from grudging hate,

And with my hand I seal my true heart's love.   10

HASTINGS

So thrive I, as I truly swear the like.

KING EDWARD

Take heed to not act false before your king,

Lest He that is the supreme King of Kings

Reveal your hidden falsehood, and ensure

Each one of you to be the other's end.   15

HASTINGS

So prosper I, as I swear perfect love.

RIVERS

And I, as I love Hastings with my heart.

KING EDWARD

Madam, yourself is not exempt from this;

— Nor you, son Dorset; — Buckingham, nor you.

You have been factious one against the other.   20

— Wife, love Lord Hastings. Let him kiss your hand,

And what you do, do it without pretense.

QUEEN ELIZABETH

There, Hastings. I will never more remember

Our former hatred, so thrive I and mine.

Hastings kisses her hand

KING EDWARD

Dorset, embrace him. — Hastings, love Lord Dorset.   25

DORSET

This interchange of love, I hereby swear,

Upon my part shall be unbreakable.

HASTINGS

And so swear I.

They embrace

KING EDWARD

Now, princely Buckingham, seal thou this league

By embracing closely my wife's allies,   30

Making me happy in your unity.

BUCKINGHAM

If ever Buckingham does turn his hate

Upon your grace — although with duteous love

I now do cherish you and yours — God punish me

With hate from those whom I expect most love.   35

When I have most need to employ a friend,

And when most assurèd that he is a friend,

Deep, hollow, treacherous and full of guile

Be he unto me. This do I beg of God,

When I am lacking love of you or yours.   40

They embrace

KING EDWARD

    A pleasing cordial, princely Buckingham,

    Is this thy vow unto my sickly heart?

    But missing now our brother Gloucester here

    To seal the blessèd period of this peace.

        Enter Ratcliffe and Richard, Duke of Gloucester

BUCKINGHAM

    And just in time,   45

    Here comes Sir Ratcliffe and the Duke.

RICHARD

    Good morrow to my sovereign King and Queen,

    And princely peers, a happy time of day.

KING EDWARD

    Happy indeed, as the day we have spent.

    Gloucester, we have done deeds of charity,   50

    Made peace of enmity, fair love of hate,

    Between these prideful, wrong-enragèd peers.

RICHARD

    A blessèd labour, my most sovereign lord.

    Among this princely heap, if any here

    By false intelligence or wrong surmise   55

    Hold me a foe;

    If I unwittingly, or in my rage,

    At any time committed what causes harm,

    To those present here, I dearly desire

    To reconcile me to this friendly peace.   60

    'Tis death to me to be at enmity;

    I hate it, and desire all good men's love.

    — First, madam, I entreat true peace of you,

    Which I will purchase with my duteous service;

    — Of you, my noble cousin Buckingham,   65

    If ever any grudge were lodged between us;

— Of you and you, Lord Rivers and of Dorset,
That undeservedly have frowned on me;
   — Dukes, earls, lords, gentlemen, indeed, of all.
I do not know an Englishman alive   70
With whom my soul is any jot at odds
More than the infant that is born tonight.
I thank my God for my humility.

QUEEN ELIZABETH

A holy day shall this be kept hereafter.
I would to God all strifes were well resolved.   75
My sovereign lord, I do beseech your highness
To take our brother Clarence to your grace.

RICHARD

Why, madam, have I offered love for this,
To be so mocked in this royal presence?
Who knows not that the gentle Duke is dead?   80

(they all start)

You do him injury to scorn his corpse.

KING EDWARD

Who knows not he is dead?! Who knows he is?

QUEEN ELIZABETH

All-seeing heaven, what a world is this?

KING EDWARD

Is Clarence dead? The order was reversed.

RICHARD

But he, poor man, by your first order died,   85
And that a wingèd Mercury did bear;
Some tardy cripple could halt that command,
But came too late so saw him buried.

KING EDWARD

Who sued to me for him? Who, in my wrath,
Kneeled at my feet and bid me be advised?   90

Who spoke of brotherhood? Who spoke of love?
Who told me how the poor soul did forsake
The mighty Warwick and did fight for me?
Who told me in the field at Tewkesbury
When Oxford had me down, he rescued me   95
And said, "Dear brother, live, and be a king"?
Who told me, when we both lay in the field
Frozen almost to death, how he did wrap me
In his own garments, and did give himself,
All thin and naked, to the numb-cold night?   100
All this from my memory's brutal wrath
Sinfully plucked, and no man among you
Had so much grace to put it in my mind.
O God! I fear Thy justice will take hold
On me, and you, and mine and yours for this.   105
— Come, Hastings, help me to my chamber. —
Ah, poor Clarence!
  All but Richard, Buckingham, and Ratcliffe exit with King Edward
           and Queen Elizabeth

RICHARD

These are the fruits of rashness: marked you not
How all the guilty kindred of the queen
Look pale on hearing of Clarence's death?   110
O! They did urge it still upon the King.
God will revenge it. Come, lords, will you go
To comfort Edward with our company?

BUCKINGHAM

We wait upon your grace.
       They exit

ACT 2 ◆ SCENE 2
A ROOM IN KING EDWARD IV'S PALACE

Enter Queen Elizabeth, her hair loose, followed by Rivers and
Dorset, and the Duchess of York.

QUEEN ELIZABETH

Ah! Who shall keep me from my wail and weep,

To chide my fortune, and torment myself?

DUCHESS

What means this scene of reckless rantings?

QUEEN ELIZABETH

Edward, my lord, thy son, our king, is dead.

DUCHESS

I have bewept a worthy husband's death   5

And lived with looking on his images;

But now two mirrors of his princely portrait

Are cracked in pieces by malignant death,

And I, for comfort, have but one false glass

That grieves me when I see my shame in him.   10

Thou art a widow, yet thou art a mother,

And has the comfort of thy children left;

But death has snatched my husband from my arms

And plucked two crutches from my feeble hands,

Clarence and Edward. O, what cause have I,   15

Thine being merely a half of my moan,

To overwhelm thy woes and drown thy cries!

QUEEN ELIZABETH

Ah, for my husband, for my dear lord Edward!

DUCHESS

Alas for both, both mine, Edward and Clarence!   20

QUEEN ELIZABETH

What strength had I but Edward? And he's gone.

DUCHESS

What strengths had I but they? And they are gone.

QUEEN ELIZABETH

Was never widow had so dear a loss.

DUCHESS

Was never mother had so dear a loss.

Alas! I am the mother of these griefs.   25

Their woes are parceled; mine is general.

She for an Edward weeps, and so do I.

I for a Clarence weep, but you do not.

DORSET *(to Queen Elizabeth)*

Comfort, dear mother. God is much displeased

That you take with unthankfulness His doing.   30

RIVERS

Madam, think more, like a cautious grandmother,

Think of your son, the young prince: send straight for him;

Let him be crowned. In him your comfort lives.

Drown desperate sorrow in dead Edward's grave

And plant your joys in living Edward's throne.   35

Enter Richard, Buckingham, Hastings, and Ratcliffe

RICHARD

Sister, have comfort. All of us have cause

To wail the dimming of our shining star,

But none can halt our harms by wailing them.

— Madam my mother, I do beg your mercy;

I did not see your grace. Humbly on my knee   40

I crave your blessing.

Kneels

DUCHESS

God bless thee and put meekness in thy breast,

Love, charity, obedience and true duty.

RICHARD

    Amen.

(rising; an aside)

    That's a blessing from the bottom of a brother-filled barrel.   45

    Amen? I marvel that my mother did leave it out.

BUCKINGHAM

    You mournful princes and heart-broken peers

    That bear this heavy shared load of sorrow,

    Now cheer each other in each other's love.

    Though we have spent our harvest of this king,   50

    We are to reap the harvest of his son.

    The broken bitterness of your inflamed hates,

    But now splinted, knit and joined together,

    Must gently be preserved, cherished and kept.

    Seems good to me that with some little pomp   55

    Forthwith from Ludlow the young Prince be fetched

    Here now to London, to be crowned our King.

RIVERS

    Why with some little pomp, my Lord of Buckingham?

BUCKINGHAM

    Indeed, my lord, lest by a multitude

    The new-healed wound of malice should break out,   60

    Which would be so much the more dangerous

    By how much the kingdom is green and yet ungoverned.

RIVERS

    Yet since it is but green, it should be put

    To no apparent likelihood of breach,

    Which by too much company might be urged;   65

    Therefore I say with noble Buckingham

    That it is right that few should fetch the prince.

HASTINGS

    And so say I.

RICHARD

 Then it be so, and go we to determine

 Who they shall be rides quickly, straight to Ludlow. 70

 — Madam, and you my sister, will you go

 To give your judgements in this business?

QUEEN ELIZABETH AND DUCHESS

 With all our hearts.

Exit all but Buckingham and Richard

BUCKINGHAM

 My lord, whoever journeys to the Prince,

 For God's sake let us two not stay at home; 75

 For on the way I will find a moment,

 As prelude to the story we last talked of,

 To part the Queen's proud kindred from the Prince.

RICHARD

 My other self, my counsel's inner sanctum,

 My oracle, my prophet, my dear cousin, 80

 I, like a child, will go by your direction:

 Toward Ludlow then, for we'll not stay behind.

They exit

ACT 2 ◆ SCENE 3

A STREET NEAR THE COURT

Enter three Citizens. {Whole scene a possible future cut.}

1 CITIZEN

 Good morrow, neighbour, what is your hurry?

2 CITIZEN

 I promise you, I scarcely know myself.

 Hear you the news a-round?

3 CITIZEN

 Is the news true of good King Edward's death?

1 CITIZEN

Ay sir, it is too true, God help us all.   5

3 CITIZEN

Then, good sirs, look to see a troubled world.

1 CITIZEN

No, no, by God's good grace, his son shall reign.

3 CITIZEN

Woe to the land that's governed by a child.

2 CITIZEN

In him there is a hope of government,

1 CITIZEN

So stood the state when Henry the Sixth   10

Was crowned in Paris but at nine months old.

3 CITIZEN

Stood the state like so? No, good friends, God knows,

Then the King had virtuous uncles to protect his grace.

2 CITIZEN

O, full of danger is the Duke of Gloucester,

And the Queen's kindred so haughty and proud;   15

1 CITIZEN

Come, come, we fear the worst; all will be well.

3 CITIZEN

Untimely storms make men expect famine.

All may be well; but if God makes it so,

'Tis more than we deserve, or I expect.

2 CITIZEN

Truly, the hearts of men are full of fear.   20

3 CITIZEN

But leave it all to God.

They exit

ACT 2 ◆ SCENE 4
A ROOM IN KING EDWARD IV'S PALACE

Enter young Duke of York, Queen Elizabeth, and the Duchess of York

QUEEN ELIZABETH

Last night, I hear, they stayed at Stony Stratford,

And at Northampton they do rest tonight.

Tomorrow, or next day, they will be here.

DUCHESS

I long with all my heart to see the Prince.

I hope he is much grown since last I saw him. 5

QUEEN ELIZABETH

But I hear no. They say my son of York

Has near overtaken him in his growth.

YORK

Ay, mother, but I would not have it so.

DUCHESS

Why, my young cousin, it is good to grow.

YORK

Grandmam, one night as we did sit at supper, 10

My uncle Rivers talked how I did grow

More than my brother. "Ay," quotes my uncle Gloucester,

"Small herbs have grace; great weeds do grow apace."

Since then, it seemed I would not grow so fast

Because sweet flowers are slow and weeds make haste. 15

DUCHESS

Good faith, in fact, the saying did not hold

For him that did opine the same to thee.

He was the most wretched thing when he was young,

Took so long to grow, and so painfully slow,

That if his rule were true, he should be gracious. 20

YORK

Now by my faith, I wish I had known that.

I could have given my uncle's grace a jeer

By teasing him more aptly than he me.

DUCHESS

How, my young York? I pray you let me hear it.

YORK

Indeed, they say my uncle grew so fast   25

That he could gnaw a crust at two hours old;

Took two full years fore I could get a tooth.

Grandmam, this would have been a "biting" jest.

QUEEN ELIZABETH

Mischievous boy; beware, you are too shrewd.

DUCHESS

Good madam, be not angry with the child.   30

QUEEN ELIZABETH

Little Pitchers have large ears.

Enter a Messenger

What news?

MESSENGER

Such news, your grace, as grieves me to report.

QUEEN ELIZABETH

How does the Prince?

MESSENGER

Well, madam, and in health.   35

DUCHESS

What is thy news?

MESSENGER

Lord Rivers and Lord Grey are sent to Pomfret —

prisoners.

DUCHESS

Who has committed them?

MESSENGER

The mighty Dukes,   40

Gloucester and Buckingham.

QUEEN ELIZABETH

For what offence?

MESSENGER

The sum of all I know, I have disclosed.

Why, or for what, the nobles were committed

Is all unknown to me, my gracious queen.   45

QUEEN ELIZABETH

Ay me! I see the ruin of my house:

The tiger now has seized the gentle doe;

Insulting tyranny begins to jut

Upon the innocent and youthful throne.

Welcome destruction, blood and massacre.   50

I see, as in a map, the end of all.

DUCHESS

Accursèd and unquiet quarreling days,

How many of you have my eyes beheld?

My husband lost his life to get the crown,

And often up and down my sons were tossed   55

For me to joy and weep their gain and loss.

And now e'en with the throne, our conflicts

Clean blown over, themselves the conquerors

Make war upon themselves, brother to brother,

Blood to blood, self against self. O monstrous   60

And frantic outrage, end thy damned ire,

Or let me die, to look on earth no more.

QUEEN ELIZABETH

Come, come my boy, we will to sanctuary.

Madam, farewell.

DUCHESS

Wait, I will go with you.   65

QUEEN ELIZABETH
You have no cause.

They exit

ACT 3 ◆ SCENE 1

A STREET IN LONDON

*The Trumpets sound. Enter young Prince Edward, the Dukes of
Gloucester and Buckingham, Lord Cardinal of Canterbury, Catesby,
with others.*

BUCKINGHAM

Welcome, sweet Prince, to London, and your throne.

RICHARD

Welcome, dear cousin, king to all my thoughts.

The weary way has made you melancholy.

PRINCE

No, uncle, but our kin, jailed on the way

Have made it tedious, wearisome and heavy.   5

I want more uncles here to welcome me.

RICHARD

Sweet Prince, the untainted virtue of your years

Has not yet dived into the world's deceit.

Those uncles you wish for were dangerous;

Your grace attended to their sugared words   10

But looked not on the poison of their hearts.

God keep you from them, and from such false friends.

PRINCE

God keep me from false friends, but they were none.

RICHARD

My lord, the Mayor of London comes to greet you.

Enter Lord Mayor with others

MAYOR

God bless your grace with health and happy days.   15

PRINCE

I thank you, good my lord, and thank you all.
I thought my mother and my brother York
Would by now have met us along the way.
Fie, what a slug is Hastings, that he comes not
To tell us whether they will come or no.   20

Enter Lord Hastings

BUCKINGHAM

And just in time, here comes the sweating lord.

PRINCE

Welcome, my lord. When will our mother come?

HASTINGS

On what occasion God He knows, not I,
The Queen your mother and your brother York
Have taken sanctuary. The tender Prince   25
Would have gladly come to greet you, your grace,
But by his mother was by force withheld.

BUCKINGHAM

Fie, what devious and foolish course
Of hers is this! — Lord Cardinal, will your grace
Persuade the queen to send the Duke of York   30
Unto his princely brother presently?
— If she deny, Lord Hastings, go with him,
And from her jealous arms pluck him by force.

CARDINAL

Lord Buckingham, if my weak-tongued pleading
Can from his mother win the Duke of York,   35
Expect him here at once; but if she be deaf
To mild entreaties, God in heaven forbid
We should defy the holy privilege
Of blessed sanctuary. Not for all this land,
Would I be guilty of so deep a sin.   40

58

BUCKINGHAM

You are too senseless-obstinate, my lord,
Too ceremonious and traditional.
Weigh it as worthy of these wanton times
You break not sanctuary in seizing him.
The benefit thereof is always granted   45
To those whose dealings have deserved the place
Or those who have the wit to claim the place.
This prince has neither claimed it nor deserved it
And therefore, in my opinion, cannot have it.
Then, taking him from that that is not there   50
You break no privilege nor promise there.
Often have I heard of sanctuary men,
But sanctuary children, never till now.

CARDINAL

My lord, you did convince my mind for once.
— Come on, Lord Hastings, will you go with me?   55

HASTINGS

I go, my lord.

PRINCE

Good lords, make all the speedy haste you may.
          Exit Cardinal and Hastings and the Mayor
Say, Uncle Gloucester, if our brother come,
Where shall we remain till our coronation?

RICHARD

Your highness shall repose you at the Tower;   60
For your best health and recreation.

PRINCE

I do not like the Tower, of any place.
— Did Julius Caesar build that place, my lord?

BUCKINGHAM

He did, my gracious lord, begin that place,

Which since succeeding ages have refortified.   65

PRINCE

Is it upon record, or just repeated

Successively from age to age, he built it?

BUCKINGHAM

Upon record, my gracious lord.

PRINCE

But say, my lord, e'en were not written down,   70

Methinks the truth should live from age to age,

As 'twere repeated to all posterity,

Even to final Judgement's all-ending day.

RICHARD *(aside)*

So wise so young, they say, do never live long.

PRINCE

What say you, uncle?   75

RICHARD

I say, without record fame lives long.

Enter young Duke of York, Hastings, and Cardinal

BUCKINGHAM

Now just in time here comes the Duke of York.

PRINCE

Richard of York, how fares our loving brother?

YORK

Well, my mighty lord — now must I call you.

PRINCE EDWARD

Ay, brother, to our grief, as it is yours.   80

RICHARD

How fares our cousin, noble Lord of York?

YORK

I thank you, gentle uncle. O, my lord,

You said that idle weeds are fast in growth.

The Prince my brother has outgrown me far.

RICHARD

He has, my lord.   85

YORK

And therefore is he idle?

RICHARD

O my fair cousin, I must not say so.

YORK

Then he is more beholding to you than I.

RICHARD

He may command me as my sovereign,

But you have power in me as in a kinsman.   90

YORK

I pray you, uncle, give me this dagger.

RICHARD

What, would you have my weapon, little lord?

YORK

I would, that I might thank you as you call me.

RICHARD

How?

YORK

Little.   95

PRINCE

My Lord of York is always cross in talk.

Uncle, your grace knows how to bear with him.

YORK

You mean to bear me, not to bear with me.

— Uncle, my brother mocks both you and me.

Because that I am little, like an ape,   100

(jumping on Richard's back)

He thinks that you should bear me on your shoulders.

RICHARD *(to York)*

My lord, will't please you to get down?

61

(to the Prince)

    Myself and my good cousin Buckingham

    Will to your mother to entreat of her

    To meet you at the Tower and welcome you.   105

YORK *(to the Prince)*

    What! Will you go unto the Tower, my lord?

PRINCE

    Yes, my Lord Protector will have it so.

YORK

    I shall not sleep in quiet at the Tower.

RICHARD

    Why, what should you fear?

YORK

    O, me, my uncle Clarence's angry ghost.   110

    My grandmam told me he was murdered there.

PRINCE

    I fear no uncles dead.

RICHARD

    Nor none that live, I hope.

PRINCE

    An' if they live, I hope I need not fear.

    But come, my lord. With a heavy heart,   115

    Thinking on them, go I unto the Tower.

*   A sennet of ceremonial trumpets*

*   Exit all but Richard, Buckingham, and Catesby*

BUCKINGHAM

    Think you, my lord, this little prattling York

    Was not incensed by his scheming mother

    To taunt and scorn you thus abusively?

RICHARD

    He is all his mother's, from the top to toe.   120

BUCKINGHAM

    Well, let them be. — Come hither, Catesby.

    Thou art as deeply sworn to effect what we intend

    As closely conceal what we impart.

    Thou know our reasons, urged upon the way.

    What do you think? Is it not an easy matter   125

    To make William Lord Hastings, meet our mind

    And praise instalment of this noble Duke

    In the seat royal of this famous isle?

CATESBY

    He for his father's sake so loves the Prince

    That he will not be swayed to side against him.   130

BUCKINGHAM

    What do you think then of Stanley? Will not he?

CATESBY

    He will do all in all as Hastings does.

BUCKINGHAM

    Well then, no more but this: go, gentle Catesby,

    And from safe distance, sound thou Lord Hastings

    How he is disposed to our purpose   135

    And summon him tomorrow to the Tower

    To there discuss the coronation.

    If thou does find him amenable to us,

    Encourage him, and tell him all our reasons.

    If he be leaden, icy, cold, unwilling,   140

    Be thou so too, and so break off the talk,

    And give us notice of his inclination.

RICHARD

    Commend me to Lord Hastings. Tell him, Catesby,

    His ancient knot of dangerous adversaries

    Tomorrow will let blood at Pomfret Castle,   145

    And bid my lord, for joy of this good news,

BUCKINGHAM

Good Catesby, go effect this business soundly.

CATESBY

My good lords both, with all the care I can.

Exit Catesby

BUCKINGHAM

Now, my lord, what shall we do if we perceive

Hastings will not yield to our exploits?   150

RICHARD

Chop off his head; something we will determine.

And look when I am king, I will give thee

The earldom of Hereford and all moveable things

Whereof the King my brother was possessed.

BUCKINGHAM

I'll claim that promise at your grace's hand.   155

RICHARD

And look to have it given with all kindness.

Come, let us sup soon so that afterwards

We may duly digest our plans with care.

They exit

ACT 3 ◆ SCENE 2

OUTSIDE LORD HASTINGS' HOUSE

Enter a Messenger to Hastings' door

MESSENGER

My lord, my lord.

HASTINGS *(from within)*

Who knocks?

MESSENGER

One from the Lord Stanley.

HASTINGS *(from within)*

What is the time?

MESSENGER

Upon the stroke of four.   5

Lord Hastings opens his door

HASTINGS

Cannot my Lord Stanley sleep these tangled nights?

MESSENGER

So it appears by that I have to say.

First, he sends greetings to your noble self.

HASTINGS

What then?

MESSENGER

Then so swears your lordship that this night   10

He dreamt the boar had ripped off his head.

HASTINGS

As for his dreams, I wonder he's so simple

To trust the mockery of unquiet slumbers.

To flee the boar before the boar pursues

Is to incense the boar to follow us   15

And make pursuit where he did mean no chase.

Go, bid thy master rise and come to me,

And we will go together to the Tower,

Where he'll see Richard the boar treat us kindly.

MESSENGER

I'll go, my lord, and tell him what you say.   20

Messenger exits. Enter Catesby.

CATESBY

Many good morrows to my noble lord.

HASTINGS

Good morrow, Catesby. You are early stirring.

What news, what news, in this our tottering state?

CATESBY

It is a reeling world indeed, my lord,

And I believe will never stand upright
Till Richard wear the garland of the realm.   25
HASTINGS
How? Wear the garland? Does thou mean the crown?
CATESBY
Ay, my good lord.
HASTINGS
I'll have this crown of mine cut from my shoulders
Before I'll see that crown so foul misplaced.
But art thou sure that he does aim at it?   30
CATESBY
Ay, on my life, and hopes to find your favor
Upon his party for the gain thereof;
And thereupon he sends you this good news,
That this same very day your enemies,
The kindred of the Queen, must die at Pomfret.   35
HASTINGS
Indeed I am no mourner for that news,
Because they have always been my enemies.
But that I'll give my voice on Richard's side
To bar King Edward's heirs in true descent,
God knows I will not, even mean it death.   40
CATESBY
God keep your lordship in that gracious mind.
HASTINGS
But I shall laugh at this a year from now,
As I live to look on the tragedy
Of those who made me suffer Edward's hate.
Well, Catesby, fore a fortnight make me older,   45
I'll send some packing that yet think not on't.
CATESBY
'Tis a vile thing to die, my gracious lord,

When men are unprepared and look not for it.
HASTINGS
O monstrous, monstrous! And so it befell
Rivers and those that think themselves as safe   50
As thou and I, who, as thou know, are dear
To princely Richard and to Buckingham.
CATESBY
The princes both make a high account of you —
(aside)
For they account his chopped head on a pole.
HASTINGS
I know they do, and I have well-deserved it.   55
Lord Stanley enters
Come, Lord Stanley. Where is your boar-spear, man?
Fear you Richard and go so unprepared?
STANLEY
My lord, good morrow. — Good morrow, Catesby.
— You may jest on, but, by the Holy Cross,
I do not like how quickly Richard moves.   60
HASTINGS
My lord, I hold my life as dear as you do yours,
And never in my days, I do proclaim,
Was it so precious to me as 'tis now.
Think you, but that I know our state secure,
I would be as triumphant as I am?   65
STANLEY
The lords at Pomfret, when they rode from London,
Were jolly and supposed their states were sure,
And they indeed had no cause to mistrust;
But yet you see how soon the day turned dark.
This sudden stab of malice I must fear.   70
Pray God, I say, I prove a needless coward.

What, shall we toward the Tower? The day's begun.

HASTINGS

Come, come, I'll join you. Know you what, my lord?

Today the Queen's kindred will be dispatched.

STANLEY

They, for their truth, might better keep their heads   75

Than some that have accused them keep their hats.

Exit Lord Stanley and Catesby, as Buckingham enters

HASTINGS

What, go you toward the Tower, Buckingham?

BUCKINGHAM

I do, my lord, but long I cannot stay there.

I shall return before your lordship does.

HASTINGS

Nay, like enough, for I stay dinner there.   80

BUCKINGHAM *(aside)*

And supper too, although thou knows it not.

— Come, will you go?

HASTINGS

At your pleasure, my lord.

They exit

ACT 3 ♦ SCENE 3

YORKSHIRE: POMFRET CASTLE

Enter Rivers, escorted by Ratcliffe, to his death

RIVERS

Sir Richard Ratcliffe, let me tell thee this:

Today shalt thou behold a subject die

For truth, for duty and for loyalty.

RATCLIFFE

Quickly. The limit of your life is out.

RIVERS

O Pomfret, Pomfret! O thou bloody prison, 5
Fatal and ominous to noble peers!
Now Margaret's curse is fall'n upon our heads,
When she condemned us, Hastings, Grey and I,
For standing by when Richard stabbed her son.
Be satisfied, dear God, with my true blood, 10
And spare my sister and her princely sons.

RATCLIFFE

Make haste. The hour of death will you atone.

They exit.

ACT 3 ◆ SCENE 4

IN THE TOWER OF LONDON

Enter Buckingham, Stanley, Hastings, Bishop of Ely, and Ratcliffe

HASTINGS

Now, noble peers, the cause why we are met
Is to arrange for the coronation.
In God's name speak: when is the royal day?

BUCKINGHAM

Is all things ready for the royal time?

STANLEY

It is, and wants but nomination, my Lord Bishop. 5

ELY

Tomorrow, then, I judge a happy day.

BUCKINGHAM

Who knows the Lord Protector's mind herein?
Who's intimate with the noble Duke?

ELY

Your grace, we think, should soonest know his mind.

BUCKINGHAM

We know each other's faces; but our hearts 10

He knows no more of mine than I of yours,

— Lord Hastings, you and he are near in love.

HASTINGS

I thank his grace, I know he loves me well;

But for his purpose in the coronation,

I have not sounded him, nor he delivered   15

His gracious pleasure any way therein.

But you, my honourable lords, may name the time,

And in the Duke's behalf I'll give my voice,

Which I presume he'll take graciously.

Enter Richard, Duke of Gloucester

ELY

And just in time, here comes the Duke himself.   20

RICHARD

My noble lords and cousins all, good morrow.

I have been so long asleep, but I trust

My absence does neglect no great design

Which by my presence might have been concluded.

BUCKINGHAM

Had you not come upon your cue, my lord,   25

William, Lord Hastings, had pronounced your part —

I mean, your voice for crowning of the King.

RICHARD

Than my Lord Hastings, no man might be bolder.

His lordship knows me well, and loves me well.

— My Lord of Ely, when I was last in Holborn   30

I saw good strawberries in your garden there;

I do beseech you send for some of them.

ELY

Indeed I will my lord, with all my heart.

Exit Bishop of Ely

RICHARD

Cousin of Buckingham, a word with you.

They talk apart

Catesby has sounded Hastings in our business, 35

And finds the testy gentleman so hot

That he will lose his head before letting

His master's child, as worshipfully he terms it,

So lose the royalty of England's throne.

BUCKINGHAM

Withdraw yourself awhile. I'll go with you. 40

Exit Richard and Buckingham

STANLEY

We have not yet set down this day of triumph.

Tomorrow, in my judgment, is too sudden,

For I myself am not so well provided

As else I would be, were the day prolonged.

Enter the Bishop of Ely

ELY

Where is my lord the Duke of Gloucester? 45

I have sent for those strawberries.

HASTINGS

His grace looks so cheerful and smooth this morning.

There's some fancy or other likes him well

When that he bids good morrow with such a spirit.

I think there's never a man in Christendom 50

Can lesser hide his love or hate than he,

For by his face straight shall you know his heart.

STANLEY

What of his heart perceive you in his face

By any livelihood he showed today?

HASTINGS

Mark me, that with no man here he is offended, 55

71

For were he, he had shown it in his looks.

Enter Richard and Buckingham

RICHARD

I pray you all, tell me what they deserve
That do conspire my death with devilish plots
Of damnèd witchcraft, and that have prevailed
Upon my body with their hellish charms?   60

HASTINGS

The tender love I bear your grace, my lord,
Makes me most forward in this princely presence
To doom th' offenders, whosoe'er they be.
I say, my lord, they have deserved death.

RICHARD

Then be your eyes the witness of her evil.   65
Look how I am bewitched! Behold, mine arm
Is like a blasted sapling, withered up;
And this is Edward's wife, that monstrous witch,
That by her witchcraft thus has marked me.

HASTINGS

If she has done this deed, my noble lord —   70

RICHARD

If? Thou protector of this damned strumpet,
Talk thou to me of ifs? Thou art a traitor.
— Off with his head! Now by Saint Paul I swear
I will not dine until I see the same.
— Ratcliffe, arrest him. Look that it be done.   75

Richard exits. Ratcliffe remains with Lord Hastings

HASTINGS

Oh woe for England, not a whit for me,
For I, a fool, might have prevented this.
Stanley dreamt the boar did rip his head,
But I did scorn it and refuse to flee.

72

Three times today my richly-clad steed stumbled, 80
And started when he looked upon the Tower,
As loath to bear me to the slaughterhouse.
O Margaret, Margaret, now thy heavy curse
Is landed on poor Hastings' wretched head.

RATCLIFFE

Come, come, hurry. The Duke should be at dinner. 85
Confess quickly. He longs to see your head.

HASTINGS

O momentary grace of mortal men,
Which we more hunt for than the grace of God!

RATCLIFFE

Come, come, quickly. 'Tis pointless to delay.

HASTINGS

O bloody Richard! Miserable England, 90
I prophesy the fearful most time to thee
That ever wretched age has looked upon.
— Come, lead me to the block; bear him my head.
They smile at me that shortly shall be dead.

They exit. We hear "My Way" by the Sex Pistols into intermission

INTERMISSION

We hear "(I'm Not Your) Stepping Stone" by the Sex Pistols into
Act 3, Scene 5

ACT 3 ◆ SCENE 5

THE COURTYARD OF THE TOWER OF LONDON

Enter Richard and Buckingham in old foot soldiers' armour

RICHARD

Come, cousin, can thou quake, make pale thy colour,
Murder thy breath in middle of a word,
And then again begin, and stop again,
As if thou were distraught and mad with terror?

BUCKINGHAM

    Tut, I can imitate the deep tragedian,   5

    Speak, and look back, and pry on every side,

    Tremble and start at a finger wagging,

    Pretending deep suspicion. Ghastly looks

    Are at my service, like enforced smiles,

    And both are ready waiting to be used,   10

    At any time to grace my strategies.

    But what, is Catesby gone?

RICHARD

    He was, and see, he brings the Mayor along.

             Enter the Lord Mayor and Catesby

BUCKINGHAM

    Lord Mayor —   15

RICHARD

    Look to the draw-bridge there!

BUCKINGHAM

    Hear that?! A drum!

RICHARD

    Catesby, look over the walls!

             Exit Catesby

BUCKINGHAM

    Lord Mayor, the reason we have sent —   20

RICHARD

    Look back! Defend thee! Here are enemies.

BUCKINGHAM

    God and our innocence defend and guard us.

             Enter Ratcliffe, with Hastings's head

RICHARD

    Be patient. Ratcliffe is a friend.

RATCLIFFE

    Here is the head of that ignoble traitor,

The dangerous and duplicitous Hastings. 25

RICHARD

So dear I loved the man that I must weep.

I took him for an honest harmless creature

That breathed upon the earth a Christian;

So smooth he plastered his vice with show of virtue.

BUCKINGHAM

Well, well, he was the most covert hidden traitor 30

That ever lived.

Would you imagine, or almost believe,

Were it not that by divine protection

We live to tell it, that the sneaky traitor

This day had plotted, in the Council House, 35

To murder me and my good Lord of Gloucester?

MAYOR

Did he so?

RICHARD

What? Think you we are Turks or infidels?

The peace of England, and our personal safety

Forced us into this execution. 40

MAYOR

Now blessings on you! He deserved his death,

And your good graces both, by this, have done well

To warn false traitors from the like attempts.

BUCKINGHAM

Had we not fast determined he should die

Before your lordship came to see his end — 45

My lord, you yourself would have heard

The traitor speak and timorously confess

The manner and the purpose of his treasons,

Then you might well have clarified the same

Unto the citizens, who perhaps may 50

Misconstrue our actions and wail his death.

MAYOR

But, my good lord, your graces' words shall serve,
As well as I had seen and heard him speak;
And do not doubt, right noble princes both,
But I'll acquaint our duteous citizens   55
With all your just proceedings in this cause.

RICHARD

And to that end we wished your lordship here,
T'avoid the doubters of this dismal world.

BUCKINGHAM

Though you came too late to see our intent,
Yet witness what you hear we did intend.   60
And so, my good Lord Mayor, we bid farewell.

Exit Lord Mayor

RICHARD

Go after, follow, cousin Buckingham.
The Mayor towards Guildhall hurries hastily
There, at your most apt and opportune time,
Allege the bastardy of Edward's children.   65
Then assert his most hateful, licentious
And bestial appetite in ways of lust,
Which stretched unto their servants, daughters, wives,
Everywhere his raging eye or savage heart,
Without control, lusted to take his prey.   70
If that is not enough to convince them:
Tell them, that when my mother was with child
With that insatiable Edward, noble York
My princely father then had wars in France,
And by true computation of the time   75
Found that this infant was not his begot,
Which well appeared in his lineaments,

Being nothing like the noble duke, my father.
Yet touch this sparingly, with far off hints,
Because, my lord, you know my mother lives.   80
BUCKINGHAM

Doubt not, my lord; I'll play the orator
As if the golden fee for which I plead
Were for myself. And so, my lord, adieu.
RICHARD

If you thrive well, bring them to Baynard's Castle.
BUCKINGHAM

I go, and towards three or four o'clock   85
Look for the news that the Guildhall provides.
RICHARD

And to command that no manner of person
Have at any time access to the princes.

Exit Richard, Buckingham, and Ratcliffe

ACT 3 ◆ SCENE 6

LONDON: THE SCRIVENER'S HOUSE

Enter a Scrivener with a paper in his hand

SCRIVENER

Here is the indictment of the good Lord Hastings.
Eleven hours, this scrivener, it took to write
But yet five hours ago Hastings lived,
Untainted, unexamined, free, at liberty.
There was a good world the while.   5
Who's so dense that cannot see this palpable device?
Yet who so dares to say he sees it not?
Bad is the world, and all will come to nought
When such ill dealing must be only thought.

Exit

ACT 3 ◆ SCENE 7

LONDON: BAYNARD'S CASTLE COURTYARD

Enter Richard and Buckingham through separate doors

RICHARD

How now, how now, what say the citizens?

BUCKINGHAM

Now by the holy Mother of our Lord,

The citizens are mum, say not a word.

RICHARD

Touched you the bastardy of Edward's children?

BUCKINGHAM

Aye, his betrothal to Lady Lucy,   5

His betrothal made by Warwick in France;

Th'insatiable greediness of his desire

And his lewd forcing of the city wives;

His tyranny for trifles; his own bastardy,

Begotten when your father was in France,   10

And his resemblance being not like the duke.

Indeed, left nothing fitting for your purpose

Untouched or slightly handled in discourse.

And when mine oratory drew toward end,

I bid them that did love their country's good   15

Cry, "God save Richard, England's royal king!"

RICHARD

And did they so?

BUCKINGHAM

No, so God help me, they spoke not a word,

But like dumb statues or breathing stones   20

Stared each on t'other and looked deadly pale.

RICHARD

What tongueless blocks were they! Would they not speak?

Will not the mayor then, and his brethren, come?

BUCKINGHAM

   The mayor is here at hand. Pretend some fear.   25

   Do not so speak unless urged strong to it;

   And look you get a prayer book in your hand,

   And stand between two churchmen, good my lord,

   For on that ground I'll make a holy hymn.

   And be not easily won to their requests;   30

   Play the maid's part: answer nay, then take it anyway.

RICHARD

   I go, and if you plead as well for them

   As I can say nay to thee for myself,

   No doubt we bring it to a happy ending.

BUCKINGHAM

   Go up to the balc'ny, the Mayor knocks.   35

       Exit Richard. Enter the Lord Mayor and Citizens

   Welcome, my lord; I await to serve here.

   I think the Duke will not be spoken with.

            Enter Catesby

   Now, Catesby, what says your lord to my request?

CATESBY

   He does entreat your grace, my noble lord,

   To visit him tomorrow, or next day.

   He is inside, with two right reverend fathers,   40

   Divinely inclined to meditation;

   And in no worldly pursuits would be moved

   To draw away from this most holy exercise.

BUCKINGHAM

   Return, good Catesby, to the gracious Duke;

   Tell him myself, the Mayor and aldermen,   45

   Are come to have some conference with his grace.

CATESBY

   I'll signify so much straight unto him.

Exits

BUCKINGHAM

    Ah ha, my lord, this prince is not an Edward.

    He is not lolling on a lewd love-bed,

    But on his knees at meditation; 50

    Not dallying with a brace of courtesans,

    But meditating with two deep divines;

    Not sleeping, to engross his idle body,

    But praying, to enrich his watchful soul.

    Happy were England, would this virtuous prince 55

    Take on his grace the sovereignty thereof.

    But sure I fear we shall not win him to it.

MAYOR

    Indeed, God forbid his grace should say us nay.

BUCKINGHAM

    I fear he will. Here Catesby comes again. 60

Enter Catesby

    Now, Catesby, what says his grace?

CATESBY

    He wonders to what end you have assembled

    Such troops of citizens to come to him,

    His grace not being warned thereof before.

    He fears, my lord, you mean no good to him. 65

BUCKINGHAM

    By heaven, we come to him in perfect love;

    And so once more return and tell his grace.

Exit Catesby

    When holy and devout religious men

    Pray at their beads, 'tis hard to draw them thence,

    So sweet is their zealous contemplation. 70

Enter Richard, from a balcony over the crowd, between two Bishops.
Then Catesby re-enters near Mayor and Buckingham.

MAYOR

   See where his grace stands, 'tween two clergymen.

BUCKINGHAM

   Two props of virtue for a Christian prince,

   To keep him from the fall of vanity;

   And see a book of prayer in his hand,   75

   True ornaments to prove a holy man.

   — Famous Plantagenet, most gracious prince,

   Lend favourable ear to our requests,

   And pardon us the interruption

   Of thy devotion and true Christian zeal.   80

RICHARD

   My lord, there needs no such apology.

   I do beseech your grace to pardon me,

   Who, earnest in the service of my God,

   Deferred the visitation of my friends.

   All that aside, what is your grace's pleasure?   85

BUCKINGHAM

   Even that, I hope, which pleases God above

   And all good men of this ungoverned isle.

RICHARD

   I do suspect I have done some offense

   That seems disgraceful in the City's eye,

   And you come to condemn my ignorance.   90

BUCKINGHAM

   Know then, it's your fault that you relinquish

   The supreme seat, the throne majestical.

   We heartily solicit

   Your gracious self to take on you the charge

   And kingly government of this your land,   95

   Not as protector, steward, substitute,

   Or lowly factor for another's gain,

But as successively from blood to blood,
Your right of birth, your dominion, your own.

RICHARD

I cannot tell if to depart in silence   100
Or bitterly to speak in your reproof
Best fits my status or your condition.
Definitively thus I answer you:
Your love deserves my thanks, but undeserved
Am I who merits not your high request.   105
First, if all obstacles were cut away,
And that my path were smoothly to the crown
As the ripe revenue and due of birth,
Yet so much is my poverty of spirit,
So mighty and so many my defects,   110
That I would rather hide me from my greatness.
The royal tree has left us royal fruit,
On him I lay that you would lay on me:
The right and fortune of his happy stars,
Which God forbid that I should wring from him.   115

BUCKINGHAM

You say Prince Edward's your brother's son;
So say we too, but by no noble wife.
Poor Elizabeth,
a care-crazed mother to many a son,
A beauty-waning and distressed widow,   120
In the afternoon of her life's middle days,
Made prize and purchase with his wanton eye.
By her, in this low-born bed begot
This Edward, whom our manners call the Prince.
Your brother's son shall never reign our king,   125
But we will plant some other in the throne
To the disgrace and downfall of your house.

And in this resolution here we leave you.

— Come, citizens. Zounds, I'll entreat no more.

Exit Buckingham and some others

RICHARD

I am unfit for state and majesty.   130

I do beseech you take it not amiss;

I cannot, nor I will not, yield to you.

CATESBY

Call him again, sweet prince; accept their suit.

If you deny them, all the land will rue it.

RICHARD

Will you enforce me to a world of cares? Call them again.   135

Exit Catesby

I am not made of stone.

Re-enter Buckingham and the rest

Cousin of Buckingham, and sage, grave men,

Since you will buckle fortune on my back,

To bear her burden, whether I will or no,

I must have patience to endure the load;   140

But if black scandal or foul-faced reproach

Ruin the outcome of your imposition,

Your mere enforcement shall thus acquit me

From all the impure blots and stains thereof,

For God does know, and you may partly see,   145

How far I am from the desire of this.

MAYOR

God bless your grace; we see it and will say it.

RICHARD

In saying so, you shall but say the truth.

BUCKINGHAM

Then I salute you with this royal title:

Long live King Richard, England's worthy king!   150

ALL

Amen.

BUCKINGHAM

Tomorrow may it please you to be crowned?

RICHARD

Even when you please, for you will have it so.

BUCKINGHAM

Tomorrow then we will attend your grace,

And so most joyfully we take our leave.　　　　　155

RICHARD

Come, let us to our holy work again.

— Farewell, my cousin; farewell, gentle friends.

They exit

ACT 4 ◆ SCENE 1

OUTSIDE THE TOWER OF LONDON

Enter Queen Elizabeth, the Duchess of York, and Lord Dorset at one
door; Anne (now Duchess of Gloucester) at another

DUCHESS

— Daughter, well met.

ANNE

God give your graces both

A happy and a joyful time of day.

QUEEN ELIZABETH

As much to you, good sister. Where do you go?

ANNE

No farther than the Tower here as I guess, 5

Upon the same devotion as yourselves,

To greet and welcome the gentle Princes there.

QUEEN ELIZABETH

Kind sister, thanks. We'll enter all together.

Enter Brakenbury the Lieutenant

And just in time, here Brakenbury comes.

Master Lieutenant, pray you, if I may, 10

How does the Prince and my young son of York?

BRAKENBURY

Right well, dear madam. By your patience,

I may not allow you to visit them.

The King strictly ordered the contrary.

QUEEN ELIZABETH

The King? Who's that? 15

BRAKENBURY

I mean the Lord Protector.

QUEEN ELIZABETH

    The Lord protect him from that kingly title.

    Has he set bounds between their love and me?

    I am their mother. Who shall bar me from them?

DUCHESS

    I am their father's mother. I will see them.   20

ANNE

    Their aunt I am in law, in love their mother,

    So bring me to their sights. I'll bear the blame.

BRAKENBURY

    No, madam, no. I may not leave it so.

    I am bound by oath, and therefore pardon me.

                  Exit Brakenbury. Enter Stanley.

STANLEY

    Let me but meet you ladies in one hour,   25

    And I'll salute your grace of York as mother

    And reverent looker-on of two fair queens.

(to Anne)

    Come, madam, you must straight to Westminster,

    There to be crowned Richard's royal queen.

QUEEN ELIZABETH

    Ah, cut my bodice open   30

    That my caged heart may have some space to beat,

    Or else I swoon with this dead-killing news.

DORSET

    Be of good cheer, Mother. Please have comfort.

QUEEN ELIZABETH

    O Dorset, speak not to me. Get thee gone.

    Death and destruction dogs thee at thy heels.   35

    Thy mother's name is ominous to children.

    If thou wilt outrun death, go, cross the seas,

    And live with Richmond, from the reach of hell.

Go fly thee, fly thee from this slaughterhouse,
Lest thou increase the number of the dead   40
And make me die a slave to Margaret's curse,
Not mother, wife, nor England's affirmed queen.

STANLEY

Full of wise care is this counsel, madam.

(to Dorset)

Take all the swift advantage of the hours.
My letters to my son-in-law, Richmond,   45
On your behalf will meet you on the way.
Be not turned tardy by unwise delay.

DUCHESS

O ill-dispersing wind of misery.
O my accursed womb, the bed of death.
Satan's spawn has thou hatched unto the world,   50
Whose unavoided stare is murderous.

STANLEY

Come, madam, come. I in all haste was sent.

ANNE

And I with all unwillingness will go.
O, would to God that the encircling edge
Of golden metal that must round my brow   55
Were red-hot steel to sear me to the brains.
Anointed let me be with deadly venom,
And die fore men can say, "God save the queen."

QUEEN ELIZABETH

Go, go, poor soul; I envy not thy glory.
To indulge me wish on yourself no harm.   60

ANNE

No? Why? When he that is my husband now
Came to me as I followed Henry's corpse,
This was my wish: "Be thou", quotes I, "accursed

For making me, so young, so long a widow;
And when thou weds, let sorrow haunt thy bed;   65
And make thy wife, if any be so mad,
More miserable by the life with thee
Than thou has made me by my dear lord's death."
Lo, fore I can repeat this curse again,
Within so small a time, my woman's heart   70
Grossly grew captive to his honeyed words
And proved the subject of mine own soul's curse,
Which until now have held mine eyes from rest;
For not even one hour in his bed
Did I enjoy the golden dew of sleep,   75
But with his fearful nightmares was often woke.
Besides, he hates me for my father Warwick,
And will, no doubt, shortly be rid of me.

QUEEN ELIZABETH

Poor heart, adieu.

DORSET

Farewell, thou woeful welcomer of glory.   80

ANNE

Adieu, poor soul, that takes thy leave of it.

DUCHESS *(to Dorset)*

Go thou to Richmond, and good fortune guide thee,

(to Anne)

Go thou to Richard, and good angels tend thee.

(to Queen Elizabeth)

Go thou to sanctuary, and good thoughts possess thee.
I to my grave, where peace and rest lie with me.   85
Eighty odd years of sorrow did I bear,
And each hour's joy wrecked with a week's despair.

QUEEN ELIZABETH

Wait, yet look back with me unto the Tower.

— Pity, you ancient stones, those tender babes
Whom envy has entombed within your walls, 90
Rough cradle for such little pretty ones;
Rude ragged nurse, old sullen playfellow
For tender princes, use my babies well.
So foolish sorrows bids your stones farewell.

They exit

ACT 4 ◆ SCENE 2

THE THRONE ROOM OF THE PALACE

The trumpets sound a sennet.
Enter the now King Richard in pomp, Buckingham, Catesby,
Ratcliffe, with other nobles and a Page.

KING RICHARD

Stand all aside. — Cousin of Buckingham.

BUCKINGHAM

My gracious sovereign.

KING RICHARD

Give me thy hand.

Richard ascends the throne, which is on a raised platform.

Trumpets sound.

Thus high, by thy advice
And thy assistance is King Richard seated. 5
But shall we wear these glories for a day?
Or shall they last, and we rejoice in them?

BUCKINGHAM

Still live they, and forever let them last.

KING RICHARD

Ah, Buckingham, now do I play touchstone 10
To test if thou be proven gold to me:
Young Edward lives; think now what I would speak.

BUCKINGHAM

Say on, my loving lord.

KING RICHARD

Why, Buckingham, I say I would be king.

BUCKINGHAM

Why so you are, my thrice-renowned liege.   15

KING RICHARD

Ha! Am I king? When young Edward still lives?

BUCKINGHAM

True, noble prince.

KING RICHARD

O bitter consequence

That Edward still should live "true noble prince"!

Cousin, thou was not wont to be so dense.   20

Shall I be plain? I wish the bastards dead,

And I would have it speedily performed.

What says thou now? Speak speedily. Be brief.

BUCKINGHAM

Your grace may do whatever pleases you.

KING RICHARD

Tut, tut, thou art all ice; thy kindness freezes.   25

Say, have I thy consent that they shall die?

BUCKINGHAM

Give me some space to breath, some pause, dear lord,

Before I definitely speak on this.

I will answer your question presently.

Buckingham exits

CATESBY *(aside to others)*

The King is angry. See, he gnaws his lip.   30

KING RICHARD *(aside)*

Ambitious Buckingham grows too watchful.

— Boy!

90

PAGE

My lord?

KING RICHARD

Knows thou not any whom corrupting gold

Will tempt into a covert deed of death?   35

PAGE

I know a discontented gentleman

Whose humble means match not his haughty spirit.

Gold were as good as twenty orators,

And will, no doubt, tempt him to anything.

KING RICHARD

What is his name?   40

PAGE

His name, my lord, is Tyrrel.

KING RICHARD

I think I know the man. Go, call him to me, boy.

Exit Page

(aside)

That shifty thinker, crafty Buckingham

No more shall be the close aide to my counsels.

Has he so long ran beside me, untired,   45

And stops he now for breath? Well, be it so.

Enter Stanley

How now, Lord Stanley, what's the news?

STANLEY

Know my loving lord,

That the Lord Dorset, as I hear, is fled

To join Richmond in France where he resides.   50

Richard dismisses Stanley. Stanley exits

KING RICHARD

Come hither, Catesby. Rumour it abroad

That Anne my wife is very grievous sick.

I will give orders to keep her hidden.

(trying to snap Catesby into action)

Look how thou dreams! I say again, spread word

That Anne my queen is sick and like to die.   55

Go do it, for it means much to my plans

To crush all hopes whose growth may damage me.

        Exit Catesby and Ratcliffe

I must wed my brother Edward's daughter,

Or else my kingdom stands on brittle glass.

Murder the princes, and marry the princess —   60

Unholy way to prosper. But I am

So steeped in blood that sin will pluck out sin.

Tear-dropping mercy dwells not in this eye.

        Enter Tyrrel

Is thy name Tyrrel?

TYRREL

James Tyrrel, and your most obedient subject.   65

KING RICHARD

Art thou indeed?

TYRREL

Try me, my gracious lord.

KING RICHARD

Dare thou commit to kill a friend of mine?

TYRREL

Please you. But I had rather kill two enemies.

KING RICHARD

Why then thou has it. Two deep enemies,   70

Foes to my rest, and my sweet sleep's disturbers,

Are they that I would have thee deal upon.

Tyrrel, I mean those bastards in the Tower.

TYRREL

Let me have open means to come to them,

And soon I'll rid you from the threat of them.   75
KING RICHARD

Thou sings sweet music. Do come closer, Tyrrel.

There is no more. Just to say it is done,

And I will love thee and reward thee for it.

TYRREL

I will dispatch them straight away.

Tyrrel exits. Enter Buckingham and Stanley

BUCKINGHAM

My lord, I have considered in my mind   80

The last request that you did sound me on.

KING RICHARD

Well, let that rest. Dorset is fled to Richmond.

BUCKINGHAM

I heard the news, my lord.

KING RICHARD

Stanley, Richmond is your wife's son. Look t' it.

BUCKINGHAM

My lord, I claim the gift, my due by promise,   85

For which your honour and your faith is pledged:

Th'earldom of Hereford and the old earl's goods

Which you have promised I shall possess.

KING RICHARD

Stanley, look to your wife; if she convey

Letters to Richmond, you'll answer for it.   90

Stanley exits

BUCKINGHAM

What says your highness to my just request?

KING RICHARD

I do remember me, Henry the Sixth

Did prophesy that Richmond should be king,

When Richmond was a little peevish boy.

A king perhaps — 95

BUCKINGHAM

My lord.

KING RICHARD

What chance the prophet could not at that time

Have told me, I being near, that I should kill him?

BUCKINGHAM

My lord, your promise for the earldom —

KING RICHARD

Richmond! When last I was at Exeter, 100

The mayor in courtesy showed me the castle

And called it Rougemont, at which name I startled

Because a bard of Ireland told me once

I should not live long after I saw Richmond.

BUCKINGHAM

My lord — 105

KING RICHARD

Ay, what's the o'clock?

BUCKINGHAM

I am thus bold to put your grace in mind

Of what you promised me.

KING RICHARD

Well, but what's o'clock?

BUCKINGHAM

Almost the stroke of ten. 110

KING RICHARD

Well, let it strike.

BUCKINGHAM

Why let it strike?

KING RICHARD

Because like a clock's hand, thou keeps striking

Between thy begging and my meditation.

I am not in the giving vein today.   115

BUCKINGHAM

May it please you to answer me my claim?

KING RICHARD

Thou troubles me; I am not in the vein.

Richard exits followed by all but Buckingham

BUCKINGHAM

And is it thus? Repays he my deep service
With such contempt? Made I him king for this?
O, let me think on Hastings and be gone   120
To Brecknock while my fearful head's still on.

Buckingham exits

ACT 4 ◆ SCENE 3

A ROOM IN KING RICHARD'S PALACE

Enter Tyrrel

TYRREL

The tyrannous and bloody act is done,
The most arch deed of piteous massacre
That ever yet this land was guilty of.
Their lips were four red roses on a stalk,
And in their summer beauty kissed each other.   5
A book of prayers on their pillow lay —
But O, by the devil — I smothered them —
This most resplendent sweet work of nature.
I could not speak, and so I left them both
To bear these tidings to the bloody King.   10

Enter King Richard

KING RICHARD

Kind Tyrrel, am I happy in thy news?

TYRREL

If to have done the thing you ordered done

Beget your happiness, be happy then,
For it is done.

KING RICHARD

But did thou see them dead?   15

TYRREL

I did, my lord.

KING RICHARD

And buried, gentle Tyrrel?

TYRREL

The chaplain of the Tower has buried them,
But where, to say the truth, I do not know.

KING RICHARD

Come to me, Tyrrel, soon at meal's sweet end,   20
When thou shalt tell the full tale of their death.
Meantime, just think how I may do thee good,
And be inheritor of thy desire.
Farewell till then.

TYRREL

I humbly take my leave.   25

Exit

KING RICHARD

The son of Clarence have I caged up close,
His daughter meanly have I matched in marriage,
The sons of Edward sleep in Abraham's bosom,
And Anne my wife has bid this world good night.
Now, I know the Breton Richmond also aims   30
At my niece Elizabeth, Edward's daughter,
And by that knot looks too close on the crown,
To her go I, a jolly thriving wooer.

Enter Ratcliffe

RATCLIFFE

My lord.

KING RICHARD

    Good or bad news, that thou comes in so bluntly?   35

RATCLIFFE

    Bad news. The Bishop is fled to Richmond,

    And Buckingham, backed with the hardy Welshmen,

    Is on the march, and still his power increases.

KING RICHARD

    The Bishop with Richmond troubles me more

    Than Buckingham and his Welsh-levied strength.   40

    Go muster men. My counsel is my shield.

    We must be brief when traitors brave the field.

They exit

ACT 4 ♦ SCENE 4

OUTSIDE KING RICHARD'S PALACE

Enter Queen Margaret

QUEEN MARGARET

    So now prosperity begins to mellow

    And drop into the rotten mouth of death.

    Here in these confines slyly have I lurked

    To watch the waning of mine enemies.

    A dire introduction do I witness,   5

    Now back to France, hoping the consequence

    Will prove as bitter, black and tragical.

    Withdraw thee, wretched Margaret. Who comes here?

Stands aside, out of sight

Enter Duchess of York and Queen Elizabeth

QUEEN ELIZABETH

    Ah, my poor princes! Ah, my tender babes,

    My unbloomed flowers, new-appearing sweets!   10

    If yet your gentle souls fly in the air

    And be not fixed in doom perpetual,

Hover about me with your airy wings
And hear your mother's lamentation.
QUEEN MARGARET *(aside)*
   Hover about her; say that right for right   15
   Hath dimmed your infant morn to agèd night.
DUCHESS
   So many miseries have cracked my voice
   That my woe-wearied tongue is still and mute.
QUEEN ELIZABETH
   Wilt thou, O God, fly from such gentle lambs
   And throw them in the entrails of the wolf?   20
   Since when did thou sleep when such a deed was done?
QUEEN MARGARET *(aside)*
   When Holy Henry died, and my sweet son.
DUCHESS
   Dead life, blind sight, poor mortal living ghost,
   Rest thy unrest on England's lawful earth,
(she sits)
   Unlawfully made drunk with innocent blood.   25
QUEEN ELIZABETH
   Ah, that thou would as soon afford a grave,
   As thou can yield a melancholy seat,
   There would I hide my bones, not rest them here.
   Ah, who has any cause to mourn but we?
                  She sits
QUEEN MARGARET *(comes forward out of hiding.)*
   If ancient sorrow be most revered,   30
   Give mine the benefit of seniority
   And let my griefs frown with an upper hand.
   If sorrow can exist with company,
   Tell over your woes again by viewing mine.
   I had an Edward, till a Richard killed him;   35

I had a husband, till a Richard killed him:
(to Queen Elizabeth)
    Thou hadst an Edward, till a Richard killed him;
    Thou hadst a Richard, till a Richard killed him.
DUCHESS *(to Queen Margaret)*
    I had a Richard too, and thou did kill him;
    I had a Rutland too; thou helped to kill him.   40
QUEEN MARGARET *(to Duchess)*
    Thou hadst a Clarence too, and Richard killed him.
    From forth the kennel of thy womb hath crept
    A hell-hound that doth hunt us all to death:
    That dog, that had his teeth before his eyes,
    Thy womb let loose to chase us to our graves.   45
    O upright, just, and true-disposing God,
    How do I thank thee that this carnal cur
    Preys on the womb's fruit of his mother's body
    And makes her pew-fellow with others' cries.
DUCHESS
    O Henry's wife, triumph not in my woes!   50
    God witness with me, I have wept for thine.
QUEEN MARGARET
    Bear with me. I am hungry for revenge,
    And now I gorge myself beholding it.
    Thy Edward he is dead, that killed my Edward,
    Young York, he is but added, because both they   55
    Matched not the high perfection of my loss.
    Thy Clarence he is dead that stabbed my Edward,
    And the beholders of this frantic play,
    The adulterous Hastings, and Rivers,
    Untimely smothered in their dusky graves.   60
    Richard yet lives, hell's black intelligencer,
    Kept alive to play Hell's agent and buy souls.

Cancel his bond of life, dear God I pray,
That I may live to say, "The dog is dead."

QUEEN ELIZABETH

O, thou did prophesy the time would come 65
That I should wish for thee to help me curse
That loathsome spider, that foul hunch-backed toad.

QUEEN MARGARET

I called thee then fake flourish of my fortune;
I called thee then, poor shadow, painted queen,
A mother only mocked with two fair babes, 70
A queen in jest, only to fit the scene.
Where is thy husband now? Where be thy brothers?
Where be thy two sons? What now dost thou joy?
Who sues, and kneels, and says, "God save the queen"?
Where be the bending peers that flattered thee? 75
Where be the thronging troops that followed thee?
Recite all this, and see what now thou art:
For happy wife, a most distressed widow;
For joyful mother, one that wails the name;
For one being sued to, one that humbly sues; 80
For queen, a piteous wretch crowned with care;
For she that scorned at me, now scorned by me;
For she being feared by all, now fearing one;
For she commanding all, obeyed by none.
Thou didst usurp my place, and dost thou not 85
Usurp the just proportion of my sorrow?
Now thy proud neck bears half my burdened yoke,
From which, even here I slip my wearied head
And leave the burden of it all on thee.
Farewell, York's wife, and queen of sad mischance. 90
These English woes shall make me smile in France.

QUEEN ELIZABETH

O thou, well skilled in curses, stay awhile
And teach me how to curse mine enemies.

QUEEN MARGARET

Forsake to sleep the night, and fast the day;
Compare dead happiness with living woe; 95
Think that thy babes were sweeter than they were,
And he that slew them fouler than he is.
Bettering thy loss makes that bad causer worse.
Pondering this will teach thee how to curse.

QUEEN ELIZABETH

My words are dull. O, sharpen them with thine. 100

QUEEN MARGARET

Thy woes will make them sharp to pierce like mine.

Queen Margaret exits

DUCHESS

Why is calamity born full of words?

QUEEN ELIZABETH

Let words break free, though what they will impart
Help nothing else, yet do they ease the heart.

DUCHESS

If so, then be not tongue-tied. Go with me, 105
And in the breath of bitter words let's smother
My damned son, that did smother thy two sweet sons.

Trumpet sounds.
Enter King Richard and his retinue, including Catesby,
marching, with Drums and Trumpets.

KING RICHARD

Who intercepts me in my expedition?

DUCHESS

O, she that might have intercepted thee,
By strangling thee in her accursed womb, 110

From all the slaughters, wretch, that thou has done.
QUEEN ELIZABETH
Hides thou that forehead with a golden crown
Where should be branded, if right were but right,
The slaughter of the prince that owned that crown
And the dire death of my poor sons and brothers? 115
Tell me, thou villain-slave, where are my children?
DUCHESS
Thou toad, thou toad, where is thy brother Clarence,
QUEEN ELIZABETH
Where are the gentle Rivers and young Grey?
DUCHESS
Where is kind Hastings?
KING RICHARD
Go strike the alarm! 120
Let not the heavens hear these telltale women
Rail on the Lord's anointed. Strike, I say!
Flourish. Alarums.
Either be patient and treat me fairly,
Or with the clamorous clatter of war
Thus will I drown your exclamations. 125
DUCHESS
Art thou my son?
KING RICHARD
Ay, I thank God, my father, and yourself.
DUCHESS
Then patiently hear my impatience.
KING RICHARD
Madam, I have a touch of your condition,
That cannot endure the sound of rebuke. 130
DUCHESS
O, let me speak.

KING RICHARD

   Do then, but I'll not hear.

DUCHESS

   I will be mild and gentle in my words.

KING RICHARD

   And brief, good mother, for I am in haste.

DUCHESS

   Art thou so hasty? I have stayed for thee,   135

   God knows, in torment and in agony.

KING RICHARD

   And came I not at last to comfort you?

DUCHESS

   No, by the Holy Cross, thou knows it well:

   Thou came on earth to make the earth my hell.

   A grievous burden was thy birth to me;   140

   Tetchy and wayward was thy infancy.

   Thy schooldays frightful, violent, wild and furious;

   Thy prime of manhood daring, bold and venturous;

   Thy present age proud, subtle, sly and bloody,

   More calm, but yet more harmful, kind in hatred.   145

   What comfortable hour can thou name

   That ever graced me with thy company?

KING RICHARD

   If I be so disgusting in your eye,

   Let me march on and not offend you, madam.

   Strike up the drum.   150

DUCHESS

   I pray thee, hear me speak.

KING RICHARD

   You speak too bitterly.

DUCHESS

   Hear me a word,

For I shall never speak to thee again.

KING RICHARD

So.   155

DUCHESS

Either thou will die by God's just ordinance

Ere from this war return a conqueror,

Or I with grief and extreme age shall perish

And never more behold thy face again.

Therefore take with thee my most grievous curse,   160

Which in the day of battle tire thee more

Than all the complete armour that thou wears.

My prayers on the opposing side's fight,

And there the little souls of Edward's children

Whisper to the ghosts of thine enemies   165

And promise them success and victory.

Bloody thou art; bloody will be thy end.

Shame serves thy life and does thy death attend.

Exits

QUEEN ELIZABETH

Though far more cause, yet much less spirit to curse

Abides in me. I say amen to her.   170

KING RICHARD

Stay, madam, I must have a word with you.

QUEEN ELIZABETH

I have no more sons of the royal blood

For thee to slaughter. For my daughters, Richard,

They shall be praying nuns, not weeping queens,

And therefore level not to wreck their lives.   175

KING RICHARD

You have a daughter called Elizabeth,

Virtuous and fair, royal and gracious.

QUEEN ELIZABETH

And must she die for this? O, let her live,

And I'll corrupt her manners, stain her beauty,

Slander myself as false to Edward's bed, 180

Throw over her the veil of infamy.

So she may live unscarred of bleeding slaughter,

I will confess she was not Edward's daughter.

KING RICHARD

Breech not her birth. She is a royal princess.

QUEEN ELIZABETH

To save her life, I'll say she is not so — 185

KING RICHARD

Her life is safest only in her birth —

QUEEN ELIZABETH

And only in that safety died her brothers —

KING RICHARD

You speak as if I had slain my cousins.

QUEEN ELIZABETH

Cousins indeed, and by their uncle cozened

Of comfort, kingdom, kindred, freedom, life. 190

My tongue should to thy ears not name my boys

Till that my nails were anchored in thine eyes.

KING RICHARD

Madam, if I thrive in my enterprise

And achieve success with this bloody war,

Then I intend more good to you and yours 195

Than ever you and yours by me were harmed.

QUEEN ELIZABETH

What good is covered by the face of heaven,

Yet to be uncovered, can do me good?

KING RICHARD

Th'advancement of your children, gentle lady.

QUEEN ELIZABETH

Up to some scaffold, there to lose their heads.   200

KING RICHARD

Even all I have — ay, and myself and all —

Will I withal endow a child of thine;

If in the Lethe River of forgetting

Thou drown thy angry soul in underworld's water

Washing off sad remembrance of those wrongs   205

Which thou supposes I have done to thee.

QUEEN ELIZABETH

Be brief, lest the telling of thy kindness

Last longer than thy kindness itself.

KING RICHARD

Then know that from my soul I love thy daughter.

QUEEN ELIZABETH

Yes thou does love my daughter from thy soul;   210

As from thy soul's love did thou love her brothers,

And from my heart's love I do thank thee for it.

KING RICHARD

Be not so hasty to confound my meaning:

I mean that with my soul I love thy daughter

And do intend to make her Queen of England.   215

QUEEN ELIZABETH

Well then, who does thou mean shall be her king?

KING RICHARD

Even he that makes her queen. Who else should be?

QUEEN ELIZABETH

What, thou?

KING RICHARD

Even so. How think you of it?

QUEEN ELIZABETH

How canst thou woo her?   220

KING RICHARD

That would I learn of you,

As one being best acquainted with her humour.

QUEEN ELIZABETH

And will thou learn of me?

KING RICHARD

Madam, with all my heart.

QUEEN ELIZABETH

Send to her, by the man that slew her brothers,   225

A pair of bleeding hearts; thereon engrave

"Edward" and "York". Then perhaps she will weep.

And then present to her — as sometimes Margaret

Did to thy father, steeped in Rutland's blood —

A handkerchief, which say to her did drain   230

The purple sap from her sweet brother's body,

And bid her wipe her weeping eyes with it.

If this inducement move her not to love,

Send her a letter of thy noble deeds:

Tell her thou made away her uncle Clarence,   235

Her uncle Rivers, ay, and for her sake

Made quick removal of her good aunt Anne.

KING RICHARD

Say that I did all this for love of her.

QUEEN ELIZABETH

Nay, then indeed she cannot choose but hate thee,

Having bought love at such a bloody cost.   240

KING RICHARD

Look what is done cannot be now amended.

Men shall deal unadvisedly sometimes,

Which after-hours gives leisure to repent.

If I did take the kingdom from your sons,

To make amends, I'll give it to your daughter.   245

A grandmam's name is little less in love
Than is the doting title of a mother.
Your children were vexation to your youth,
But mine shall be a comfort to your age.
The loss you have is but a son being king,   250
And by that loss your daughter is made queen.
Go then, my mother; to thy daughter go.
Prepare her ears to hear a wooer's tale;
And when this arm of mine has chastised
The petty rebel, dull-brained Buckingham,   255
Bound with triumphant garlands will I come
And lead thy daughter to a conqueror's bed;
To whom I will recount my conquest won,
And she shall be sole victoress, Caesar's Caesar.

QUEEN ELIZABETH
What were I best to say? Her father's brother   260
Would be her lord? Or shall I say her uncle?
Or he that slew her brothers and her uncles?
Under what title shall I woo for thee,
That God, the law, my honour and her love
Can make seem pleasing to her tender years?   265

KING RICHARD
Imply fair England's peace by this alliance —

QUEEN ELIZABETH
Which she shall purchase with eternal war —

KING RICHARD
Tell her the King, that may command, does beg —

QUEEN ELIZABETH
That which the King's Almighty King forbids —

KING RICHARD
Say I will love her everlastingly —   270

QUEEN ELIZABETH

But how long shall that title "ever" last?

KING RICHARD

As long as heaven and nature lengthens it —

QUEEN ELIZABETH

As long as hell and Richard likes of it —

KING RICHARD

Be eloquent on my behalf to her —

QUEEN ELIZABETH

An honest tale works best being plainly told —   275

KING RICHARD

Then plainly to her tell my loving tale —

QUEEN ELIZABETH

Plain and not honest is too harsh a style —

KING RICHARD

Your reasons are too shallow and too quick —

QUEEN ELIZABETH

O no, my reasons are too deep and dead,

Two deep and dead, poor infants, in their graves.   280

KING RICHARD

Harp not on that string, madam; that is past —

QUEEN ELIZABETH

Harp on it still shall I, till heartstrings break —

KING RICHARD

I swear by —

QUEEN ELIZABETH

Swear then by something thou has not wronged.

KING RICHARD

Then by myself —   285

QUEEN ELIZABETH

Thyself is self-misused.

KING RICHARD

Why then, by God —

QUEEN ELIZABETH

God's wrong is most of all.

If thou had feared to break an oath to Him,

Th'imperial metal circling now thy head   290

Had graced the tender temples of my child,

And both the princes had been breathing here,

Which now, two tender bed-fellows for dust,

Thy broken faith has made them prey for worms.

What can thou swear by now?   295

KING RICHARD

The time to come.

QUEEN ELIZABETH

That thou has wronged in the time now past;

The children live whose fathers thou has slaughtered,

The parents live whose children thou has butchered.

KING RICHARD

As I intend to prosper and repent,   300

So thrive I in my dangerous affairs

Of hostile arms. Myself myself destroy!

Heaven and fortune halt my happy hours.

Day, yield me not thy light; nor, night, thy rest.

Be opposite all planets of good luck   305

To my proceeding, if with dear heart's love,

Immaculate devotion, holy thoughts,

I do not win thy beauteous princely daughter.

In her exists my happiness and thine;

Without her what follows for myself, thee,   310

Herself, the land and many a Christian soul,

Death, desolation, ruin and decay.

Therefore, dear mother — I must call you so —

Be the attorney of my love to her:
Urge the necessity and state of times,   315
And be not foolish when in great designs.

QUEEN ELIZABETH

Shall I be tempted by the devil thus?

KING RICHARD

Ay, if the devil tempt you to do good.

QUEEN ELIZABETH

Yet thou did kill my children —

KING RICHARD

But in your daughter's womb I bury them.   320

QUEEN ELIZABETH

Shall I go win my daughter to thy will?

KING RICHARD

And be a happy mother by the deed.

QUEEN ELIZABETH

I go, write to me very shortly,
And you shall understand from me her mind.

KING RICHARD

Bear her my true love's kiss; and so farewell.   325

Exit Queen Elizabeth

Relenting fool, and shallow, changing woman.

Enter Ratcliffe and Catesby

How now, what news?

RATCLIFFE

Most mighty sovereign, on the western coast
Anchors a powerful navy. To our shores
Throng many no doubt cowardly friends,   330
Unarmed and unresolved to beat them back.
'Tis thought that Richmond is their admiral,
And there they drift, expecting but the aid
Of Buckingham to welcome them ashore.

KING RICHARD

Some light-foot friend ride to the Duke of Norfolk: 335

Ratcliffe, thyself — or Catesby. Where is he?

CATESBY

Here, my good lord.

KING RICHARD

Catesby, fly to the Duke.

CATESBY

I will, my lord, with all convenient haste.

KING RICHARD

Ratcliffe, come here. Ride to Salisbury. When thou gets there — 340

(to Catesby)

Dull unmindful villain,

Why stay thou here, and go not to the Duke?

CATESBY

First, mighty liege, tell me your highness' pleasure,

What from your grace shall I deliver to him.

KING RICHARD

O true, good Catesby. Bid him now levy   345

The greatest strength and power that he can make

And meet me with great haste at Salisbury.

CATESBY

I go.

Exits

RATCLIFFE

What, may it please you, shall I do at Salisbury?

KING RICHARD

Why, what would thou do there before I go?   350

RATCLIFFE

Your highness told me I should ride before.

KING RICHARD

My mind is changed.

Enter Lord Stanley

Stanley, what news with you?

STANLEY

None good, my liege, to please you with the hearing,

Nor none so bad but well may be reported. 355

KING RICHARD

Hey now, a riddle! Neither good nor bad.

What need thou run so many miles about

When thou may tell thy tale the nearest way?

Once more, what news?

STANLEY

Richmond is on the seas. 360

KING RICHARD

There let him sink, and be the seas on him,

White-livered renegade. What does he there?

STANLEY

I know not, mighty sovereign, but by guess.

KING RICHARD

Well, as you guess?

STANLEY

He makes for England, here to claim the crown. 365

KING RICHARD

Is the chair empty? Is the sword unswayed?

Is the King dead? The empire unpossessed?

What heir of York is there alive but we?

And who is England's king but great York's heir?

Then tell me, what does he upon the seas? 370

Thou will revolt and fly to him, I fear.

STANLEY

No, my good lord; therefore mistrust me not.

KING RICHARD

Where is thy army then, to beat him back?

Are they not now upon the western shore,

Safe-conducting the rebels from their ships?   375

STANLEY

No, my good lord, my friends are in the north.

KING RICHARD

Cold friends to me. What do they in the north

When they should serve their sovereign in the west?

STANLEY

They have not been commanded, mighty King.

If pleases your majesty to give me leave,   380

I'll muster up my friends and meet your grace

Where and what time your majesty shall please.

KING RICHARD

Ay, thou would be gone to join with Richmond,

But I'll not trust thee.

STANLEY

Most mighty sovereign,   385

You have no cause to hold my friendship doubtful;

I never was, nor never will be, false.

KING RICHARD

Go then, and muster men, but leave behind

Your son George Stanley. Look your heart be firm,

Or else his head's security is but frail.   390

STANLEY

So deal with him as I prove true to you.

Exit Stanley. Enter a Messenger.

1 MESSENGER

My gracious sovereign, now in Devonshire,

Sir Edward Courtney and the proud prelate,

Bishop of Exeter, his elder brother,

With many more confederates are in arms.   395

Enter another Messenger

114

2 MESSENGER

    In Kent, my liege, the Guildfords are in arms,

    And every hour more associates

    Flock to the rebels, and their power grows strong.

Enter another Messenger

3 MESSENGER

    My lord, the army of great Buckingham —

KING RICHARD

    Out on you, owls! Nothing but songs of death.   400

He strikes him

    There, take thou that, till thou bring better news.

3 MESSENGER

    The news I have to tell your majesty

    Is that by sudden floods and waterfalls

    Buckingham's army is dispersed and scattered,

    And he himself wandered away alone,   405

    No man knows to where.

KING RICHARD

    I cry thee mercy.

    There is my purse to cure that blow of thine.

Enter Catesby

CATESBY

    My liege, the Duke of Buckingham is taken.   410

    That is the best news. That the Earl of Richmond

    Is with a mighty army landed at Milford

    Is colder tidings, but yet they must be told.

KING RICHARD

    Away towards Salisbury! While we reason here

    A royal battle might be won and lost.   415

    Someone take order Buckingham be brought

    To Salisbury. The rest march on with me.

Flourish of trumpets. Exit.

ACT 4 ◆ SCENE 5

THE HOUSE OF STANLEY, EARL OF DERBY

Enter Stanley and a Messenger

STANLEY

Young fellow, please tell Richmond this from me:

That in the sty of the most deadly boar

My son George Stanley is penned up and held;

If I revolt, off goes young George's head.

The fear of that holds off my present aid.   5

So get thee gone. Commend me to thy lord.

Also, say that the Queen has heartily consented

Richmond should marry Elizabeth her daughter.

But tell me, where's that princely Richmond now?

MESSENGER

At Pembroke or at Ha'rfordwest in Wales.   10

STANLEY

Well, speed thee to Richmond. I kiss his hand.

My letter will resolve him of my mind.

Farewell.

They exit

ACT 5 ♦ SCENE 1

SALISBURY: A PLACE OF EXECUTION

Enter Buckingham, led to execution by the Sheriff and Halberds

BUCKINGHAM

Will not King Richard let me speak with him?

SHERIFF

No, my good lord; therefore be quiet.

BUCKINGHAM

Hastings, and Edward's children, Grey and Rivers,

Holy King Henry, and thy fair son Edward,

And all those that have been murdered   5

By underhand, corrupted, foul injustice,

If now your wrathful, discontented souls

Do through the clouds behold this present hour,

Take your revenge and mark my destruction.

— This is All Souls' Day, fellow, is it not?   10

SHERIFF

It is.

BUCKINGHAM

Why, then All Souls' Day is my body's doomsday.

This is the day which, in King Edward's time,

I wished might fall on me if ever I was found

False to his children or his wife's allies.   15

This is the day on which I was betrayed

By the false faith of him whom most I trusted.

This, this All Souls' Day to my fearful soul

Is the determined righting of my wrongs:

Thus Margaret's curse falls heavy on my neck: 20

"When he", quotes she, "shall split thy heart with sorrow,

117

Remember Margaret was a prophetess."
— Come, lead me, officers, to the block of shame.
Wrong has but wrong, and blame the due of blame.

They exit.

ACT 5 ◆ SCENE 2
TAMWORTH: THE CAMP OF RICHMOND

Enter Richmond, Oxford, Blunt, and others, with Drums and
Standardbearers

RICHMOND

Fellows in arms, and my most loving friends,
Bruised underneath the yoke of tyranny.
Here receive we from our father Stanley
Words of fair comfort and encouragement.
The wretched, bloody and usurping boar,   5
Swills your warm blood like slop, and makes his trough
In your emboweled bosoms, this foul swine
Is now squarely in the center of this isle,
Near to the town of Leicester, as we learn.
In God's name, march with cheer, courageous friends,   10
To reap the harvest of perpetual peace
By this one bloody trial of fierce war.
True hope is swift and flies with eagle's wings;
Kings it makes gods, and meaner creatures kings.

Exit all

ACT 5 ◆ SCENE 3
BOSWORTH FIELD

Enter King Richard with Norfolk and Ratcliffe dressed for battle

KING RICHARD

Here pitch our tent, just here in Bosworth field.
Here will I lie tonight.

Soldiers begin to set up Richard's tent

But where tomorrow? Well, never mind that.

Who has found out the number of the traitors?

NORFOLK

Six or seven thousand is their utmost number.   5

KING RICHARD

Why, our battalion triples that account.

Besides, the King's name is a tower of strength,

Which they on the opposite faction lack.

Let's lack no discipline, make no delay,

For lords, tomorrow is a busy day.   10

Richard's tent is ready. Richard and his retinue exit

Enter Richmond and Blunt with Dorset and Oxford

RICHMOND

The weary sun has made a golden set,

And by the bright track of his fiery cart

Gives a sign of a goodly day tomorrow.

— Give me some ink and paper in my tent;

I'll draft the plan and model for our battle,   15

Captain Blunt, where is Lord Stanley quartered?

BLUNT

His regiment lies half a mile at least

South from the mighty army of the King.

RICHMOND

If without peril it be possible,

Sweet Blunt, make some good means to speak with him.   20

BLUNT

Upon my life, my lord, I'll undertake it,

And so God give you quiet rest tonight.

RICHMOND

Good night, good Captain Blunt.

Exit Blunt

Come, gentlemen,
Into my tent; the dew is raw and cold. 25

Exit Richmond's camp

Enter Richard's camp

KING RICHARD

What is't o'clock?

CATESBY

It's suppertime, my lord; it's nine o'clock.

KING RICHARD

I will not sup tonight. Give me some ink and paper.
Good Norfolk, speed thee to thy charge,
Use careful watch, choose trusty sentinels. 30

NORFOLK

I go, my lord.

Exit Norfolk

KING RICHARD

Catesby.

CATESBY

My lord.

KING RICHARD

Send a messenger from our forces
To Stanley's regiment. Bid him bring his army 35
Before sun-rising, lest his son George fall
Into the blind cave of eternal night.

Exit Catesby

Fill me a bowl of wine. Light a watch-candle.
Saddle white Surrey for the field tomorrow.
— Ratcliffe. 40

RATCLIFFE

My lord.

KING RICHARD

Give me another bowl of wine.

I have not that liveliness of spirit
Nor cheer of mind that I was wont to have.
(wine is brought by a servant)
Ratcliffe, about the mid of night come to my tent   45
And help to arm me. Leave me, I say.
    Exit Ratcliffe with others. Richard goes into his tent to sleep.
      Enter Stanley, and other Lords, to Richmond's tent.

STANLEY

Fortune and Victory sit on thy helm.

RICHMOND

All comfort that the dark night can affor
Be to thy person, my noble stepfather.
Tell me, how fares our loving mother?   50

STANLEY

I, by proxy, bless thee from thy mother,
Who prays continually for Richmond's good.
In brief, for so the time does bid us be,
Prepare thy soldiers early in the morning
And put thy fortune to the fearless test   55
Of bloody strokes and fatal-staring war.
At my first chance, will I disguise intent
And aid thee in this dreadful clash of arms.
But on thy side I may not be too forward,
Lest, if seen, thy half-brother, tender George,   60
Be executed 'fore my weeping eyes.
Farewell, Richmond; be valiant and succeed.

RICHMOND

Good lords, conduct him to his regiment.
I'll strive with troubled thoughts to take a nap,
Lest leaden slumber weigh me down tomorrow   65
When I should mount with wings of victory.
Once more, good night, kind lords and gentlemen.

Exit all but Richmond

(a prayer)

O God, whose captain I account myself,

Look on my forces with a gracious eye;

Put in their hands Thy righteous bruising wrath,   70

That we may praise Thee in the victory.

Sleeping and waking, O, defend me still!

Richmond sleeps.

The lights cross to Richard's tent. As Richard sleeps, he dreams of the
Ghosts of Henry VI, Clarence, Rivers, the Princes, Hastings, Lady
Anne, and Buckingham, which surround his bed. Richard trembles
in his sleep. The Ghost of Henry the Sixth, speaks first.

GHOST OF HENRY VI

I, true King Henry, made to bleed by you,

Condemn you, you counterfeit king!

The Ghost of Clarence speaks

GHOST OF CLARENCE

I that was washed to death with sick-sweet wine,   75

Poor Clarence, by thy guile betrayed to death.

The Ghost of Rivers speaks

GHOST OF RIVERS

Think on Rivers beheaded at Pomfret,

When thy brain spills, as thy soul despairs.

The Ghosts of the Princes speak

GHOSTS OF PRINCES *(speaking in unison)*

Dream on thy nephews smothered in the Tower.

Let us weigh thee down to ruin, shame and death.   80

The Ghost of Lady Anne, Richard's wife, speaks

GHOST OF LADY ANNE

Richard, thy wife, that wretched Anne, who slept

Unquiet with thee, fills thy sleep with fears.

The Ghost of Buckingham speaks

GHOST OF BUCKINGHAM

The first was I that helped thee to the crown;

The last was I that felt thy tyranny.

The Ghost of Hastings speaks

GHOST OF HASTINGS

Bloody and guilty, guiltily awake,   85

Think on your beheading of Lord Hastings.

The Ghost of Buckingham speaks

GHOST OF BUCKINGHAM

Think on, think on, of Buckingham and death

Despair in bloody battle, yield thy breath.

Richard cries out in his sleep

The Ghosts smile and nod, turn to Richmond and speak

GHOST OF HENRY VI

Be cheerful, Richmond. Angels for you sing.

I, Henry, prophesied thou shouldst be king,   90

GHOST OF CLARENCE

House of Lancaster, the heirs of York pray

Good angels guard thy battle on this day.

GHOST OF RIVERS

When you awake you will conquer the fray.

GHOSTS OF PRINCES

Richmond, sleep now in peace and wake in joy.

GHOST OF LADY ANNE

Dream of success and happy victory.   95

GHOST OF HASTINGS

God's good angels fight on Richmond's side,

Let Richard fall from grace due to his pride.

GHOST OF BUCKINGHAM

Quiet, untroubled soul, when you awake,

Arm, fight, and conquer, for fair England's sake.

ALL THE GHOSTS *(to Richmond)*

 Richmond, live and flourish!   100

(turning back to Richard, they speak in a round, echoing one another)

 Richard, let us sit heavy on thy soul at dawn.

 Despair and die, oh, Satan's darkest spawn.

    Richard starts up out of a dream,

    dispersing the ghosts into the shadows

KING RICHARD

 Give me another horse! Bind up my wounds!

 Have mercy, Jesu. — Soft, I did but dream.

 O coward conscience, how dost thou afflict me!   105

 The lights burn blue. It is now dead midnight.

 Cold fearful drops stand on my trembling flesh.

 What do I fear? Myself? There's none else here.

 Richard loves Richard, that is, I am I.

 Is there a murderer here? No. Yes, I am.   110

 Then fly! What, from myself? Great reason why?

 Lest I revenge. What, myself upon myself?

 But no, I love myself. Wherefore? For any good

 That I myself have done unto myself?

 O, no. O, no, I rather hate myself,   115

 For hateful deeds committed by myself.

 I am a villain. Yet I lie; I am not.

 Fool, of thyself speak well. Fool, do not flatter.

 I shall despair. There is no creature loves me,

 And if I die, no soul will pity me.   120

 And wherefore should they, since that I myself

 Find in myself no pity to myself?

    Enter Ratcliffe

RATCLIFFE

 My lord.

KING RICHARD

Zounds, who is there?

RATCLIFFE

Ratcliffe, my lord, 'tis I. The early village cock   125

Has twice done salutation to the morn;

Your friends are up and buckle on their armour.

KING RICHARD

O Ratcliffe, I have dreamed a fearful dream!

Methought the souls of all that I had murdered

Came to my tent, and every one did threat   130

Tomorrow's vengeance on the head of Richard.

What think thou, will our friends prove all true?

RATCLIFFE

No doubt, my lord.

KING RICHARD

O Ratcliffe, I fear, I fear.

RATCLIFFE

Nay, good my lord, be not afraid of shadows.   135

KING RICHARD

By the Apostle Paul, shadows tonight

Have struck more terror to the soul of Richard

Than can the substance of ten thousand soldiers

Iron-clad, and led by shallow Richmond.

'Tis not yet near day. Come, go with me.   140

Under our tents I'll play the eavesdropper,

To see if any mean to shrink from me.

Exit Richard and Ratcliffe

Enter Lord Oxford to Richmond's tent

LORD OXFORD

Good morrow, Richmond.

RICHMOND

Cry mercy, lord and watchful gentleman,

That you have taken a tardy sluggard here.   145
LORD OXFORD

How have you slept, my lord?
RICHMOND

The sweetest sleep and fairest-boding dreams

That ever entered in a drowsy head.

Methought the souls whose bodies Richard murdered

Came to my tent and cried out victory.   150

I promise you my soul is very joyful

In the remembrance of so fair a dream.

How far into the morning is it, Oxford?
LORD OXFORD

Upon the stroke of four.
RICHMOND

Why, then 'tis time to arm and give direction.   155

(his oration to his soldiers)

Loving countrymen, remember this:

God, and our good cause, fight upon our side.

Except Richard, those whom we fight against

Had rather have us win than him they follow.

For, what is he they follow? Truly, gentlemen,   160

A bloody tyrant and a murderer!

Then in the name of God and all our rights,

Advance your standards, sound drums and trumpets

For God, Saint George, Richmond, and victory!

Exit Richmond and his followers

Enter King Richard, Ratcliffe, and Soldiers

KING RICHARD

Who saw the sun today?   165
RATCLIFFE

Not I, my lord.

KING RICHARD

  Then he disdains to shine, for by the book

  He should have braved the east an hour ago.

  A black day will it be to somebody.

  Ratcliffe!   170

RATCLIFFE

  My lord?

KING RICHARD

  The sun will not be seen today.

  The sky does frown and glower upon our army.

  I would these dewy drops weren't on the ground.

  Not shine today? Why, what is that to me   175

  More than to Richmond? For the selfsame heaven

  That frowns on me looks sadly upon him.

                    Enter Norfolk

NORFOLK

  Arm, arm, my lord! The foe flaunts in the field.

KING RICHARD

  Come, bustle, bustle. Harness well my horse!

  — Call up Lord Stanley; bid him bring his forces.   180

  — I will lead forth my soldiers to the plain,

  And thus my battle shall be ordered:

  My front line shall be drawn out all in length,

  Consisting equally of horse and foot;

  Our archers shall be placed in the midst.   185

  John, Duke of Norfolk, Thomas, Earl of Surrey,

  Shall be the leaders of this foot and horse.

  They thus directed, we will follow

  In the main battle, whose power on either side

  Shall be flanked by our best mounted soldiers.   190

  This, and Saint George to boot. What thinks thou, Norfolk?

NORFOLK

A good direction, warlike sovereign.

(he shows him a paper)

This found I on my tent this morning:

"Johnnie of Norfolk, be not so bold,

For Dickie thy master is bought and sold." 195

KING RICHARD

A ploy devised by the enemy.

— Go, gentlemen, every man unto his charge.

Let not our babbling dreams affright our souls.

Conscience is but a word that cowards use,

Devised at first to keep the strong in awe. 200

Our strong arms be our conscience, swords our law.

March on, join bravely, let us to it pell-mell,

If not to heaven, then hand in hand to hell.

(his oration to his army)

Remember whom you are to fight against,

Assorted vagabonds, rascals and runaways, 205

A scum of Bretons and base lackey peasants!

And who does lead them but a paltry fellow?

A milksop, one that never in his life

Felt so much cold as over shoes in snow.

If we be conquered, let men conquer us. 210

And let not these bastard Bretons,

Enjoy our lands?! Lie with our wives?!

Ravish our daughters?!

(drum sounds from afar)

Lo, I hear their drum.

Fight, gentlemen of England! — Fight, bold yeomen! 215

— Draw, archers, draw your arrows to the head!

— Spur your proud horses hard, and ride in blood.

Amaze the Heavens with your broken lances.

Enter a Messenger

— What says Lord Stanley? Will he bring his army?

MESSENGER

My lord, he does deny to come.   220

KING RICHARD

Off with his son George's head!

NORFOLK

My lord, the enemy is past the marsh:

After the battle let George Stanley die.

KING RICHARD

A thousand hearts are great within my bosom.

Advance our standards! Set upon our foes!   225

Our ancient word of courage, fair Saint George,

Inspire us with the ire of fiery dragons.

Upon them! Victory sits on our helms.

They exit

ACT 5 ◆ SCENE 4
BOSWORTH: THE BATTLEFIELD

Alarum, excursions. Enter Norfolk with soldiers, and Catesby

CATESBY

Rescue, my Lord of Norfolk. Rescue, rescue!

The King enacts more wonders than a man,

Goading the enemy to every danger.

His horse is slain, and all on foot he fights,

Seeking for Richmond in the throat of death.   5

Exit Norfolk and soldiers. Alarums. Enter King Richard.

KING RICHARD

A horse, a horse, my kingdom for a horse!

CATESBY

Withdraw, my lord. I'll help you to a horse.

KING RICHARD

Slave, I have thrown my life on fate's dice,

And I accept the hazard of the die.

I think there be six Richmonds in the field;   10

Five have I slain today instead of him.

A horse, a horse, my kingdom for a horse!

They exit.

ACT 5 ◆ SCENE 5
THE ACTION CONTINUES AT BOSWORTH
THE BATTLEFIELD

Alarum, Enter King Richard and Richmond; they fight.
Richard is slain defending himself fiercely. Richmond's men all fall
upon the corpse of Richard and stab him multiple times.
A trumpet sounds retreat. Exit Richmond. Richard's body is
removed. Flourish. Enter Richmond, Stanley, bearing the crown,
with other Lords and Soldiers.

RICHMOND

God and your arms be praised, victorious friends:

The day is ours; the bloody dog is dead.

STANLEY

Courageous Richmond, well has thou earned this crown.

(presents the crown)

Lo, here this long-usurped royalty

From the dead temples of this bloody wretch   5

Have I plucked off to grace thy noble brows.

Wear it, enjoy it and make much of it.

RICHMOND

Great God of heaven, say amen to all.

But tell me, is young George Stanley living?

STANLEY

He is, my lord, and safe in Leicester town.   10

RICHMOND

Proclaim a pardon to the soldiers fled
That in submission will return to us;
And then, as we have taken the sacrament,
We will unite the white rose and the red.
Smile heaven upon this fair conjunction,   15
That long have frowned upon their enmity.
What traitor hears me and says not amen?
England has long been mad and scarred herself —
The brother blindly shed his brother's blood.
All this divided York and Lancaster,   20
Divided in their dire division.
O, Richmond and Princess Elizabeth,
The true succeeders of each royal house,
By God's fair ordinance join together;
Enrich the time to come with smooth-faced peace.   25
Now civil wounds are stopped; peace lives again.
That she may long live here, God say amen.

ALL

Amen.

END until …

EPILOGUE

RICHARD III (from Richard's text in HENRY VI, Part 3)

*Richard's Ghost walks on and speaks. Henry VII/Richmond and
Stanley and the other characters hear him, especially Queen
Margaret and Queen Elizabeth. "London's Burning" by the Clash,
is interspersed between Richard's spoken lines, we hear a phrase, as
if the music is orchestrating his words. Everyone other than Richard
strikes a pose as if caught in strobe lights when the music plays.*

RICHARD

Amen, say I, crippled by my cruel life

Now pierced by Richmond's Judas-knife.
I was born to haunt this dark monarchy.
Hist'ry has led me to this anarchy.

(music)

For this amongst the rest, was I ordained.
For mankind, always violence has reigned.   5

(music)

Down, down to hell; and say I sent thee there:
I, that have neither pity, love, nor fear.

ALL THE OTHERS *(falling to the ground)*

"O, Jesus bless us, he is born with teeth!"

RICHARD

I have no brother, I am like no brother;
And this word "love," in all you sheep-like men   10
But not in me: I am myself alone.

(music)

Thy turn is next, and then the rest,
Counting myself but bad till I be best.

ALL THE OTHERS *(rising from the floor)*

With other face will he to us return
To haunt our dreams and make them crash and burn.   15

Music turns up, Richard, the others, and his band, dance wildly,
until Richard knocks over his mic stand, breaks a guitar,
something bloody and violent.
The others exit. Richard leaves through the audience.

BLACKOUT
END OF PLAY